BIRDS OF CANADA

BIRDS OF CANADA

TEXT

John Gooders

PAINTINGS

Maurice Pledger
Trevor Boyer

DRAWINGS

Robert Morton

DESIGN

Grant Bradford

DRAGON'S WORLD

Dragon's World Ltd
High Street
Limpsfield
SURREY RH8 0DY
Great Britain

Designed by Grant Bradford

ISBN: 0 905895 39 8
D. L. TO: 1291 -1984
Printed in Spain by Artes Graficas Toledo S.A.

On page 141 the European Tree Sparrow is
shown along with the House Sparrow.
Though not a Canadian bird this old world
species has been successfully introduced to
the St. Louis area of Missouri and adjacent
parts of Illinois and may well spread
northwards into Southern Ontario in the
future, Similarly on page 109 the European
Jack Snipe is depicted alongside the
Common Snipe to show how similar these
two birds are. A single bird was shot at
Makkouik Bay, Labrador on Christmas Eve
1927.

CONTENTS

Introduction

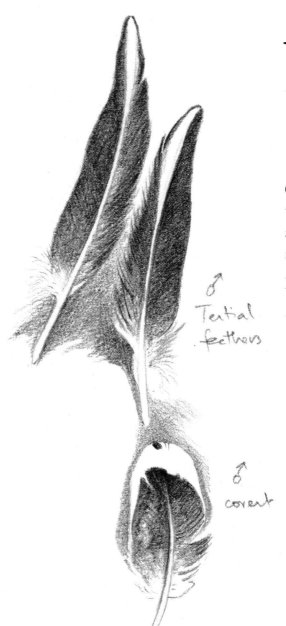

♂
Tertial
feathers

♂
covert

Canada is a country that, even as we draw toward the end of the twentieth century, still finds a great deal of its natural assets intact. There remain great tracts of forest where man seldom ventures, vast marshes where nature reigns supreme, and magnificent mountains where we simply stand and stare. Wilderness is now regarded as valuable and in this respect Canada can offer more than most. In forests, marshes and mountains wild animals still exist in numbers that are the envy of many other nations. Fish proliferate and attract anglers from all over the world, while even the non-fisherman wants to see for himself the incredible run of salmon along the rivers of the Pacific. Of birds there are plenty and for many species Canada offers the safest of breeding grounds.

No less than four hundred and thirty bird species are regularly recorded in Canada and another hundred or so are of less regular appearance. They breed from the prairies, through the conifer and birch forests, to the tundra beyond; from Vancouver in the west to Newfoundland in the east. Everywhere there are birds. With such a wealth to choose from it is not surprising that books covering them all are rare and illustrated books rarer still. To paint detailed portraits of all the birds of Canada would be a lifetime's work so, not surprisingly, a choice has had to be made.

In making this selection, therefore, we know that we cannot please everyone. Perhaps some of our readers would have chosen more birds of prey, others more wildfowl, and others still would wish we had room for the woodpeckers and the warblers, for gulls and terns, and for shorebirds. What has been done, however, is to choose a cross section of the more spectacular of Canadian birds. Wildfowl, including the Canada Goose; birds of prey including the magnificent but rare Bald Eagle; and gamebirds including the splendid Ruffed Grouse are the mainstays of the book. There are abundant birds like the Barn Swallow and rare ones like the Prairie Chicken. There are native birds like the poorly named Winter Wren and introduced ones like the ubiquitous

Starling. There are large birds like the Golden Eagle and tiny ones like the Golden-crowned Kinglet. If nothing else, this book shows the variety of the birds of Canada.

Though man has lived in Canada for a long, long time it is only over the past hundred and fifty years or so that he has actually altered the landscape. So far the changes wrought have had little effect on birdlife, though this is more true of species that breed in the north than those that were never more than on the edge of their range in the south. Now perhaps there are signs of a more significant change. Today more and more people are wanting to enjoy the wilderness, to experience nature and to share its delights. Popular sites may sometimes be inundated with visitors, while other, equally attractive areas, are deserted. In general, though, there are a greater number of visitors to wilderness areas than ever before, and the number continues to grow as urban man seeks a wider understanding of the countryside. Many habitats are very fragile and easily damaged, and when we destroy a habitat we also destroy the plants, animals and birds that live there.

The birds of Canada are part of the natural heritage, and one that should not, and must not, be taken for granted.

Canada Goose

The thrilling cackle of geese overhead and the sight of dramatic skeins across the spring and fall sky conjures up a taste of the wilderness for most Canadians. Each spring thousands of birds fly northwards over our towns and farmsteads to their breeding grounds among the ice floes and meltwater beyond the Arctic Circle. Some stop-over at a favored lake or marsh along the way gives us a chance to feel the excitement of birds on migration. Soon they are gone.

Later, in the fall, they return, their numbers swollen by the young birds that have hatched out among the wilderness. Their journey now is more leisured and they pause at stop-overs for a week or more, often feeding on the corn specially grown to attract them to safe wildfowl refuges.

Most numerous of all are the Canada Geese, a bird familiar to every Canadian, as well as to people all over the world. In eastern Canada these are indeed birds of the arctic, though from Manitoba westwards they also breed right across the prairies and Rockies south to the United States border and beyond. But this is truly a Canadian bird, with by far the world's largest numbers breeding within our borders.

The Canada is large in comparison with other geese, though it varies considerably in size. Large birds measure forty-three inches overall with a wingspan of seventy-two inches; while smaller birds may be no more than twenty-two inches overall with a wingspan of forty-eight inches. These variations in size have prompted ornithologists to recognize several distinct forms or subspecies, and some have even suggested that there may be more than one species of Canada Goose. All, however, share the same basic plumage pattern. The head and neck are black, broken by a bold white patch extending from the chin to the nape. The brown upperparts are boldly barred with creamy-buff and the flight feathers are dark brown. The underparts are creamy on the breast, becoming darker and heavily barred on the belly, while the rear end and undertail coverts are pure white, terminating in a black tail. Feet and bill are large and black.

Canada Goose
Branta canadensis

Canada Geese are gregarious at all seasons and even form loose colonies on their breeding grounds with nests no more than five yards apart. Yet they are far from friendly and, in winter flocks, birds spend an inordinant amount of time in dispute with their neighbors. Males defend a territory around their mate and season's offspring and continually attack or threaten other males that invade their domain. Mostly this takes the form of head pumping and various head postures often accompanied by loud calls, hissing and foot trampling. Such disputes are particularly common during pair formation and it seems that winter flocks are dominated by the largest family parties.

At the start of the breeding season family parties are broken up by parental hostility towards the young of the previous season; and at this time yearling birds form a pair-bond that will last for the rest of their lives. Some of these early relationships come to grief, but once a pair is finally settled, usually in the second year, the birds remain faithful to one another as long as they live. If one member dies a new mate is quickly found, but then too faithfulness is the rule.

10

The nest is constructed on the ground mostly by the female of whatever materials are within reach – usually grasses, leaves and reeds. It is situated near water, often on a lake island or promontory and lined with down plucked from her own breast. The five to seven white eggs are laid singly each day, or every other day, and are covered with down and vegetation until the clutch is complete. If a clutch is lost it will be replaced, but only one brood is ever raised.

Incubation, which lasts from twenty-eight to thirty days is by the female alone, though the male is always close at hand and frequently stands guard close to his sitting mate. The young chicks all hatch at about the same time, certainly within twenty-four hours, and are covered in brown and yellow down. They quickly leave the nest for the safety of water, but spend the night ashore being brooded by the female. They can feed themselves from the start, but are tended and defended by both members of the pair.

After three weeks much of the yellow coloration has faded and the chicks become grayer in color. It takes some forty to forty-eight days before they can fly. While the young goslings are growing the adults pass into molt and soon lose all of their wing feathers. Thus for a period each year the whole population is completely flightless. When parent and young can both fly the family party gathers together with other families and sets off southwards on the long migration down the continent. They stay together as a unit throughout their journey and through the winter until the spring. Young birds then break away on their own and form non-breeding flocks until they too settle down to nesting at three years of age.

Through their vast range across the whole of North America Canada Geese vary enormously in size as well as in coloration. The largest are found in southern Manitoba and have a whitish patch on the forehead. The smallest, in contrast, are migrants to the coast of British Columbia and have a creamy-buff, not white, face patch and often a small white collar. More important, perhaps, this latter form has a much smaller bill than most other Canada Geese, indicating that it prefers different food. In other parts of Canada various forms are found and it is interesting to pick out the differences in a local

population. Canada Geese feed entirely on vegetable matter, mainly grazing on dry land. They take grass, roots, tubers and seeds as well as large quantities of aquatic plants and crops such as wheat, rice, oats, barley, sorghum and soybeans, depending on local abundance. They also feed in water and frequently up-end like ducks.

Over the past three hundred years Canada Geese have been introduced to Europe, especially to Britain. At first their numbers were small and they remained at, or close to, the site of introduction – often a country park. More recently they have increased and spread and are now quite numerous throughout Britain as well as in Sweden and a single area of Norway. The British birds have lost their migratory habits, though there are indications that a molt-migration northwards in fall is becoming established. Swedish birds, however, migrate south westwards to Germany and Holland and a ringed bird has been recovered in Spain. To many Britons the sight and sound of wild geese overhead is no more than folklore, but now the introduced Canada Goose is bringing a touch of the wild even to great centers of population like London.

Shoveler

Shoveler are among the most attractive and distinctive of Canadian duck. The large spatula-shaped bill is a highly specialized form of the normal surface-feeding duck bill, with a broad tip and a series of hair-like serrations that act as a highly efficient filter system.

When Shoveler are feeding they usually sweep the bill from side to side, sucking in huge quantities of water and filtering out small planktonic animals and plants. In this they closely resemble the unfortunately rare Roseate Spoonbill of the southern United States, though many related surface-feeding duck such as Mallard and Green-winged Teal also filter feed to some extent.

Sometimes several Shoveler feed together, following each other in circles, head to tail like elephants at a circus. This probably stirs up the water bringing small crustaceans and molluscs, as well as insects and larvae, to the water's surface. On one occasion a pair of Shoveler were watched feeding continuously in the same spot for an hour and a half.

Females

Male in
eclipse

Of course, such intensive feeding is only available in Canada during the rich bloom of life in the summer months, so, not surprisingly, Shoveler are almost entirely summer visitors to the Canadian parts of their range. They are most numerous in the west, extending from the Yukon and western Mackenzie to Saskatchewan, but they also breed along the shores of Lakes Erie and Ontario as well as along the St Lawrence River to New Brunswick.

In the fall they move southwards to south and western United States, Mexico, coastal Central America and the West Indies, though some remain within our borders to winter in south-western British Columbia. During these winter months they sometimes gather into quite large flocks, though usually only at roosts. At other times they are spread out over the splashy marshes and lakes where they find their food. In general these flocks are peaceable, but in spring when pairing takes place the males may be highly aggressive in defence of their territories and mates. Mostly such aggression takes the form of vigorous head pumping in which the crown feathers are depressed, the bill held slightly uptilted and the head repeatedly raised and lowered. This performance is accompanied by a distinctive *took* call uttered out of sync with the head movements.

Shoveler
Anas clypeata

Close encounters or mock fights are also frequent, particularly early in the breeding season at territorial boundaries. Two adjacent males will then repeatedly jump over each other with wings flailing and splashing the water in a tight circle, though without really making any actual contact. Real fights involving pecking at neighbors do occur, but are much less frequent than the mock battles. Males seldom fight females and females seldom fight each other.

Shallow, reed-fringed lakes are the preferred habitat at all seasons and these are generally rather small, or backwaters of larger lakes. The nest is hidden among waterside vegetation though sometimes among heather or scrub some distance from water. The female constructs the nest from materials found within bill reach of the nesting hollow and lines it with warm down. The eggs vary from buff to pale olive-green and number nine or ten, rarely six to eight, and seldom eleven or more. When the clutch is complete the female incubates alone for twenty-two or twenty-three days, although some males stay nearby during the earlier stages. Only one brood is reared, however replacement clutches are laid if a first clutch is lost. The chicks, which have large bills, even when they first emerge from the eggs, are clothed in brown and buff down and leave the nest together soon after hatching. They can feed themselves, but are cared for by the female who broods them while they are small and defends them against predators. They can fly at forty to forty-five days old and then become independent.

In juvenile plumage they closely resemble the female and, for a period in late summer while the males are in eclipse plumage molting, all Shoveler look much the same in shades of brown and buff. Juvenile males then pass through a 'supplementary' plumage that is a scruffy version of the adult's before gaining full adult male plumage in the spring after they hatch. They breed at one year old.

Marsh Hawk
&
Shoveller

Drake Shoveler stand out at considerable distances by virtue of their shining white breasts. The head appears black, though a close approach shows it to have a dark bottle-green gloss. The back is black and white and the underparts bright chesnut, obvious both on the water and in flight. Females closely resemble the females of other surface-feeding duck, though they are usually more warmly colored on the breast. In both sexes the huge spatulate bill is a prominent field mark both at rest and in flight. They vary in size from seventeen to twenty and a half inches.

Elsewhere Shoveler breed right around the Northern Hemisphere. The European population moves south and westward, but large numbers fly south to East Africa, the Middle East, India and China.

19

Mallard

One of Canada's, and indeed the world's, most successful ducks, the Mallard is just as at home on park ponds in city centres as it is on the wild marshes of the far north-west. It is a very adaptable bird indeed, capable of living in virtually any type of aquatic habitat and even resorting to the sea on occasion. It is, of course, this adaptability that has enabled it to prosper and become probably the world's most widespread and numerous species of wildfowl.

Yet despite its commonness the male is still a bird to be admired. The bill is bright yellow and the head a shiny bottle-green. A narrow neck-ring of white borders the chocolate-brown breast which forms a distinct dark band that is particularly obvious in flight. Back and flanks are both delicate shades of gray, with the central back feathers a contrasting black. The tail is black with white outer feathers and the upper tail coverts curl upwards distinctively. Though Mallard have been widely domesticated and many different forms have been bred from them, the curly tail feathers have invariably been retained and show their wild ancestry.

The female is a mottled brown and buff bird like other female surface-feeding duck. There is a prominent eyebrow and eyestripe and in flight she shows the same distinctive blue and white speculum – the bold pattern of color which most ducks have on their inner wings – as the male. She also has white outer tail feathers that form a sure means of separating Mallard from Black Duck. They vary in size from 19½ to 25½ inches.

Mallard breed right across Canada from the area of Montreal and the mouth of the St Lawrence westwards

Mallard
Anas platyrhynchos

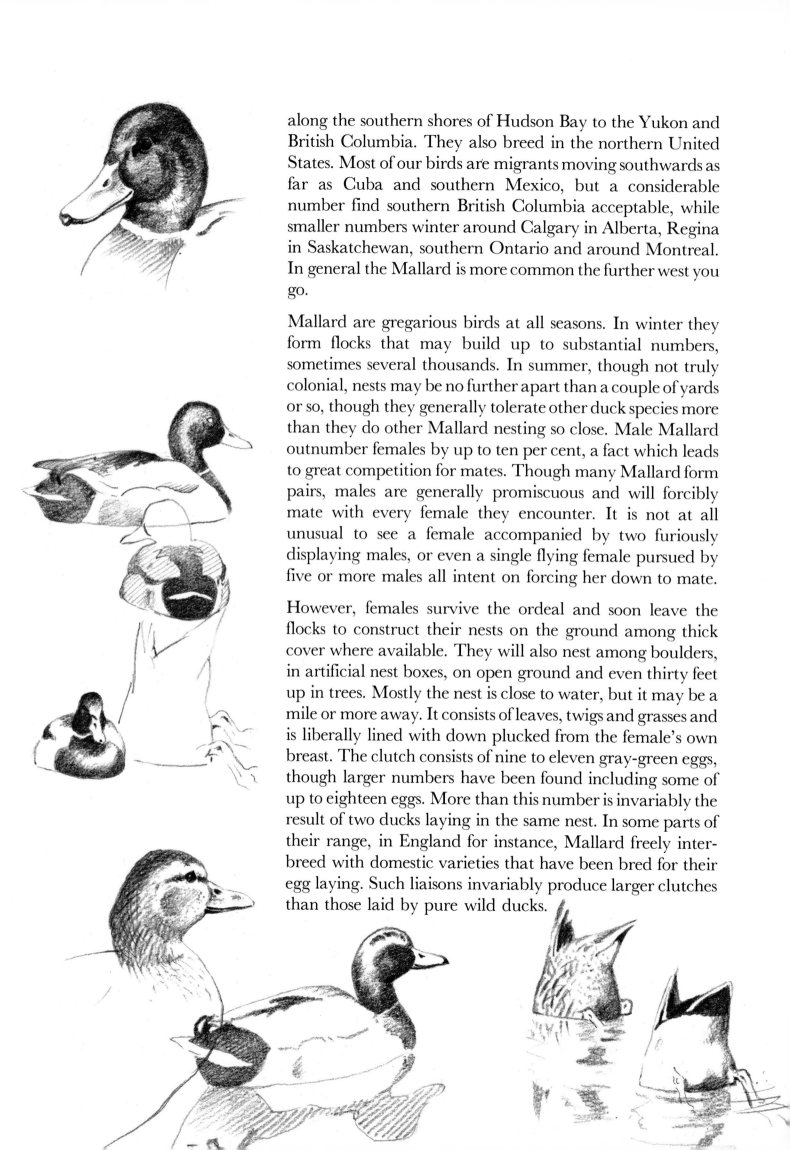

along the southern shores of Hudson Bay to the Yukon and British Columbia. They also breed in the northern United States. Most of our birds are migrants moving southwards as far as Cuba and southern Mexico, but a considerable number find southern British Columbia acceptable, while smaller numbers winter around Calgary in Alberta, Regina in Saskatchewan, southern Ontario and around Montreal. In general the Mallard is more common the further west you go.

Mallard are gregarious birds at all seasons. In winter they form flocks that may build up to substantial numbers, sometimes several thousands. In summer, though not truly colonial, nests may be no further apart than a couple of yards or so, though they generally tolerate other duck species more than they do other Mallard nesting so close. Male Mallard outnumber females by up to ten per cent, a fact which leads to great competition for mates. Though many Mallard form pairs, males are generally promiscuous and will forcibly mate with every female they encounter. It is not at all unusual to see a female accompanied by two furiously displaying males, or even a single flying female pursued by five or more males all intent on forcing her down to mate.

However, females survive the ordeal and soon leave the flocks to construct their nests on the ground among thick cover where available. They will also nest among boulders, in artificial nest boxes, on open ground and even thirty feet up in trees. Mostly the nest is close to water, but it may be a mile or more away. It consists of leaves, twigs and grasses and is liberally lined with down plucked from the female's own breast. The clutch consists of nine to eleven gray-green eggs, though larger numbers have been found including some of up to eighteen eggs. More than this number is invariably the result of two ducks laying in the same nest. In some parts of their range, in England for instance, Mallard freely inter-breed with domestic varieties that have been bred for their egg laying. Such liaisons invariably produce larger clutches than those laid by pure wild ducks.

Incubation, which is performed by the female alone, lasts for twenty-seven or twenty-eight days starting when the clutch is complete. Some males stand guard for a day or two at the beginning, but most are away busily pursuing other females. When the female leaves the nest to feed she covers the eggs with down. The ducklings hatch within twenty-four hours of each other and then leave the nest to feed themselves in a tightly knit group that the female defends and broods. The brown and buff ducklings take some fifty to sixty days to fly and become independent. Though only one brood is reared, the female will readily replace lost clutches and frequently breed again if the whole brood is lost while still young. Mallard have an extraordinarily lengthy breeding season, though less so in Canada than in more southerly parts of their range. Late breeders may either be birds that have lost their previous brood, or birds that were born early in the spring and are first breeding at the age of six or seven months.

Mallard are a prime hunting target and over half of all birds that successfully fledge will die each year. Despite such pressure they continue to thrive, mainly because they are so adaptable.

Mallard and Peregrine

23

Green-winged Teal

Teal are small, fast-flying, gregarious and attractive little duck that often behave like shorebirds by performing tightly controlled aerial acrobatics. Flocks, a hundred or more strong, twist first this way and then that in perfect formation and without so much as a single collision. Then, just as suddenly as they took off, they land again, either on the water or along some marshy shoreline.

Like most of our wildfowl, Teal are only summer visitors to Canada, though some do winter in south-western British Columbia. Most pass southwards to winter in the United States, though birds do range as far south as Cuba and Central America. In other parts of the world they breed right across Europe and Asia, from France to the Pacific coast of the USSR. These birds too are migrants moving southwards to Africa, India, China and the Philippines, though large numbers also winter in Western Europe. These Old World birds belong to the nominate subspecies *Anas crecca crecca*, whereas the birds that breed throughout North America belong to the subspecies *Anas crecca carolinensis* known as the Green-winged Teal. As a matter of fact both subspecies have green in the wing and our bird is so-called to distinguish it from the Blue-winged Teal that breeds right across Canada in much the same areas as the Green-winged.

Male Teal are delightful birds. The head is chestnut with a large bold patch of green on the sides bordered by a narrow yellow line before and below the eye. The breast is mottled buff and the back and flanks are pale gray separated by a line of black along the edge of the wing. A vertical white line divides the breast from the flanks. The tail is black with a characteristic triangular patch of yellowish-buff on each side. The female is mottled in buffs and browns like other female surface-feeding duck and is best identified by its small size and in flight by a narrow white wing bar.

Green-winged Teal
Anas crecca

Teal found in the Old World differ appreciably only in the male where the yellow lines bordering the green head patch are more continuous. They also have a white and black, not just black line along the edge of the wing and lack the white vertical line between breast and flanks. The females differ hardly at all and are inseparable in the field. These minor differences in the males are, however, sufficient to encourage birders on both sides of the Atlantic to check out each Teal they see in the hope of discovering one that should be on the other side of the ocean. Thus the Green-winged Teal is classed as a rare vagrant to Europe, while the Common Teal has been discovered on a number of occasions in North America including several in Canada. Mostly these birds have been shot by hunters and one such bird shot in Newfoundland in 1925 was a female that had been banded in England.

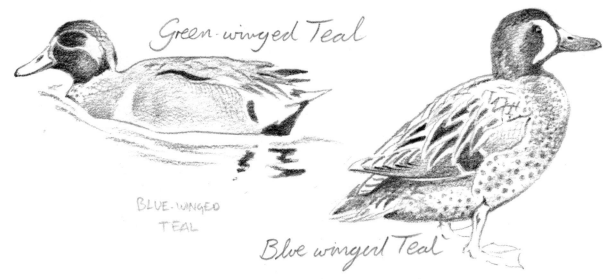

Green-winged Teal

BLUE-WINGED
TEAL

Blue winged Teal

Though Teal are most often found on or beside fresh water, they are abundant among coastal marshes and regularly use large estuaries and, to a lesser extent, other intertidal areas. In winter they adopt a regular routine of gathering at a safe roost, often in huge numbers, by day and then flighting out each evening to feed under cloak of darkness. Their food consists mostly of seeds taken from mud covered by a few inches of water. Usually, feeding birds swim with head underwater, though they also walk with a typically rolling gait, swinging the bill from side to side like a Shoveler. Less frequently Teal up-end like Mallard, scoop food from the water's surface and occasionally dive. Most food consists of seeds of sedges and other aquatic vegetation. Grain is seldom taken because the seeds are too large. In summer animal food is also taken depending on abundance.

Teal form pairs during the winter while still remaining in large flocks. The pair then remain faithful until the end of their respective breeding duties, which in the case of the male means the onset of incubation. As with so many wildfowl species the duties of nest building, incubation and care of the young devolves entirely on the female. Pair formation is a communal affair with several, up to twenty-five though usually no more than seven, males displaying to a single female. Mostly these are unpaired birds, but male Green-winged Teal regularly leave their mates to participate. Throughout the displays the males are very vocal, uttering such special courtship calls as *zee-zee-zeet*; *prip-prip*; *krik-et*; and *te-teu-te*. These displays have been given such names as Burp-display, Water-flick, Head-up-tail-down and so on, and make much use of head pumping and spreading the wings

and tail to reveal their colors. Though the practice is not as prevalent as among Mallard, male Teal will sometimes force themselves on females and on occasion such rapes have led to the female drowning.

The female builds her nest of leaves and grass lined with down in the shelter of a tussock and well hidden from view. Sometimes nests can be found within a yard of each other. The eight to eleven yellowish eggs are replaced if lost, but only one brood is reared. The female incubates for twenty-one to twenty-three days and the down-covered chicks leave the nest soon after hatching and feed themselves. The female stands guard and broods her young while they are still small, at which time they may return to the nest during the night. The young ducklings can fly after twenty-five to thirty days and are then independent of the female. They breed when one year old.

Like so many wildfowl the end of the breeding season sees a complete molt that involves the male adopting a special eclipse plumage. Then, for a period of about a month, all birds shed their primaries and are completely flightless relying on their camouflaged plumage to protect them against predators.

Green-winged Teal breed right across Canada from the Yukon to Newfoundland. They are absent from the northern North West Territories and most of the Arctic islands, but also from interior and northern Quebec, though they have been found nesting at Ungava Bay. Over the rest of Canada they breed wherever conditions are right and regularly pass through lakes that are unsuitable for breeding on their long journies north and south.

European Wigeon

The high pitched, whistling call of European Wigeon as they flight out over the falling tide of a lonely estuary is one of the most characteristic and evocative sounds of European wetlands. Huge flocks gather to winter among the saltings and splashy fields making this one of the most numerous of winter wildfowl. Unfortunately this attractive duck is generally no more than a rare visitor to Canada, though small numbers now winter along the coast of British Columbia from the end of October through March.

Elsewhere in Canada European Wigeon are decidedly rare, though more eager birders; increasingly aware of the possibility of sighting such a visitor; are finding waifs from across the ocean. There is even a record of breeding, though this was apparently a case of mistaken identity. So those who wish to see this attractive little duck in Canada must make a winter trip to B.C.

The male Wigeon is a delightfully well marked bird and easily identifiable, even at considerable distances. The head is a bright chestnut marked by a slash of gold over the crown. The chestnut terminates in a clear-cut line at the base of the neck and the breast is a warm buffy-pink. The back and flanks are pale gray separated by a narrow white line, while the black tail is long and pointed. This is particularly noticeable in flight and is reminiscent of the tail of Pintail, though not as long. Between the gray flanks and black tail is a prominent patch of white that can be picked out at surprising distances over the muddy wastes of winter estuaries.

American Wigeon

Female.

Gyr Falcon
preying on
American Wigeon

The female is a duller bird altogether, with buff, brown and chestnut barring and only a slight pale line along the flanks. In general it is less mottled and more rufous than the females of other surface feeding duck, though in structure it bears a close resemblance to the female American Wigeon. Both species have small heads and bills, though the female American Wigeon has a gray not brown head – the major difference between females of the species.

In flight the male European Wigeon shows a prominent white patch on the inner forewing that flashes clearly. American Wigeon show the same mark. In both species the female shows only a palish patch that is easily missed.

European Wigeon are seldom found far from water. They are principally grazers and find most of their food on saltings or on nearby grassland. They are particularly fond of flooded grassland and then occur well inland provided there is a sufficiently large area of water nearby to act as a safe roost. In their grazing habits they often occur alongside various species of geese and almost every area that holds these larger birds will certainly also hold good numbers of Wigeon.

European Wigeon
Anas penelope

Pairs are established quite early in the winter among the flocks and are then generally maintained through to the end of incubation. The bond between the pair is strong and there is little evidence of the promiscuity found in other surface feeding ducks such as Mallard. After northward migration in spring the pairs leave the flocks and choose a nesting lake in open, lightly wooded areas. Like the American Wigeon, and unlike most other duck, courtship is extremely vocal.

The female constructs the nest of whatever materials are at hand and forms a neat cup with various twists and turns of her body. The nest is usually well hidden among scrub, over-hanging vegetation or a grass tussock. The eight or nine creamy-buff eggs are incubated by the female for twenty-four or twenty-five days, starting when the clutch is complete. Replacement clutches may be laid if the original clutch or brood is lost. The male is frequently nearby, but moves away toward the end of incubation and takes no further part in the proceedings. The chicks hatch within a few hours of each other and are led away from the nest by the female. They are clothed in cream and brown down and feed themselves from the start. The female guards and cares for them during the forty to forty-five days they take to fledge. The young birds are independent as soon as they can fly, sometimes a little earlier.

At the end of the breeding season females and juveniles join the rafts of molting males prior to migration. These molting grounds are usually along the main migration routes, are usually along the main migration routes, sometimes near the breeding grounds, but often quite long distances away. Then in fall the birds move out to their winter quarters. In Europe these are mainly in Britain and Ireland and involve a westerly movement from Scandinavia that, in poor weather, may take birds out over the Atlantic to make an eventual landfall on the east coast of North America. As a result there have been several ringing recoveries in eastern Canada.

Elsewhere, Wigeon breed right across Eurasia from Scotland to northern Japan. All are highly migratory and large numbers winter through the Middle East to India, China and Japan. Many birds fall prey to hunters, both on migration and in winter, and of the hordes that set out in fall only about half will return the following spring. Nevertheless the number of Wigeon seems to remain much the same and there has even been an extension of range in Britain where it first bred in 1834.

The birds that winter in British Columbia doubtless originate from the eastern Siberian population and their regularity gives some hope that eventually these birds may start breeding on the American side of the Bering strait, perhaps in Canada itself.

Golden Eagle

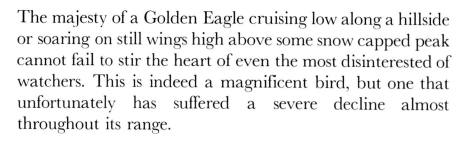

The majesty of a Golden Eagle cruising low along a hillside or soaring on still wings high above some snow capped peak cannot fail to stir the heart of even the most disinterested of watchers. This is indeed a magnificent bird, but one that unfortunately has suffered a severe decline almost throughout its range.

Since man invented the shotgun and hunting became a fashionable sport an endless war has been waged against all birds of prey. In most cases this persecution has been pointless and stupid, for the vast majority of birds of prey do no harm whatsoever to stocks of game. In the case of the Golden Eagle things are not so clear cut. The bird undoubtedly takes numbers of gamebirds, but only where such birds are abundant. So it is a balance between losing the Eagle or losing a few quarry – most people would, I am sure, prefer the latter.

In other parts of the world, Eagles have been accused of killing lambs, an offence that does little to endear them to hard pressed hill farmers. No doubt the birds do eat lambs, but usually only as carrion after they have died naturally. This is, however, a very powerful predator that does on occasion take sickly lambs as well as young deer and even young caribou. Over most of their range Golden Eagles take whatever prey is locally abundant and most easily obtained. In some areas it is mostly gamebirds, in others small mammals and in others still carrion forms the largest part of the diet.

In Canada the Golden Eagle has disappeared from large parts of the more settled east and is now common only in the Rockies and north. It is resident over great areas, though even the Eagle cannot find enough food to sustain it in the Yukon, Northwest Territories or northern Quebec. Birds that breed there move southwards to winter across the border in the northern and central United States.

Golden Eagles are far from being exclusively North American birds, however. They range right across Europe, North Africa, Turkey and the Middle East, and from Siberia to the

Golden Eagle
Aquila chrysaetos

Himalayas, China and Japan. Most are resident, though the central Siberian population, like the birds of northern Canada, move southwards to milder climes in winter.

The Golden Eagle is not a difficult bird to identify. Though many identification guides stress the possibility of confusion with the various hawks (buteos), the Eagle is almost twice the size at rest and even larger in the air. It varies in size from twenty-nine to thirty-four and a half inches, and has a wingspan of up to eighty-four inches, or nearly eight feet. At any distance adults are more or less uniformly dark brown marked by progressively paler golden head and wings as the birds get older. Immatures are dark brown, but with white wing bars and white tail feathers terminating in a black band. It was these tail feathers that formed the basis of the most elaborate head-dresses of the original North American Indian chiefs. Only the Bald Eagle can really be confused with the Golden, but this bird has a white head and tail when adult. Young Bald Eagles could be confused with adult Golden Eagles, though the Golden is darker and young Bald Eagles have white in the wings. However, by far the best means of distinction, as with so many birds of prey, is structure. The Golden Eagle has a smaller head and longer tail than the Bald Eagle and this is quite obvious in flight.

Because of the long nesting season Golden Eagles start to breed early in the year, usually long before the last snows have melted. Each pair has a territory covering many square miles within which it has a variable number of established nest sites or eyries. Most pairs have about five different nest sites that may be used in different years, though a pair in Idaho had 12 sites from which to choose.

Golden Eagle
young birds at
different stages

immature birds
in flight

Nests of adjacent pairs are seldom closer than half a mile, but more usually two to three miles separate occupied eyries, sometimes up to ten miles. Though they establish so many eyries most pairs have a favored site as well as a second choice and usually work a rota between the two.

Most eyries are located on inaccessible cliffs, though seldom on the highest or most spectacular. Low outcrops are frequently favored, though an eyrie may be situated in an old tree. Being used over and over again for many years such nests often grow to huge proportions. They are constructed of twigs lined with grass and heather to which fresh green branches are added throughout the breeding season. Though the female does most of the gathering the male also brings in material. The two oval white eggs are blotched with rust and brown and are laid three or four days apart. Occasionally only one egg is laid, and rarely three, and seldom four. Though replacements for lost eggs are possible it is decidedly unusual so that nest robbers do great harm to this species.

Eagles
eyrie

Incubation, mainly by the female, starts with the first egg and the eaglets hatch at the same interval as that between laying. The resulting difference in age and size means that the elder invariably obtains the bulk of food brought to the nest, and in eighty per cent of cases persecutes its younger sibling which ultimately dies. If, however, the younger eaglet gets through the first few weeks of life, both chicks will survive quite amicably together.

The young are fed mainly by the female, though both parents bring food to the eyrie. The female also broods her young for the first few weeks of life. By thirty days the young can feed themselves and the adults spend less time at the nest frequently visiting it only to dump food. The youngsters can fly after sixty-five to seventy days, but still rely on their parents for food for a further three months. In the far north independence is achieved more quickly as young and old alike must migrate south for the winter. The immature birds do not breed until three or four years of age.

Immature Golden Eagle
on young deer

Bald Eagle

Though adopted as the symbol of the United States of America, the Bald Eagle is now decidedly more common outside the boundaries of the contiguous States. The largest population exists in Alaska, but Canada is now the home to many more Bald Eagles than can be found south of the border. Once widespread throughout North America south to Baja California, this symbol of a nation has been ruthlessly persecuted almost everywhere. It seems particularly prone to disturbance and has suffered greatly as a result. Destruction of habitat has been particularly important, but Bald Eagles seem quite unable to adapt to living closely alongside man.

Though often labeled a coward and scavenger, the Bald Eagle is actually an accomplished hunter, quite capable of existing without any carrion at all. Despite this, it is quick to take advantage of any extra source of food, however provided. It will, for example, readily pick up road casualties such as small mammals and other birds, and visit garbage dumps, but this is merely an extension of its natural behavior. Such natural scavenging can best be seen along the salmon-rich rivers of British Columbia and Alaska.

Here, most notably at the McNeil and Chilkat rivers of Alaska, several hundreds or even thousands of Bald Eagles may gather to feed on the spent salmon that litter the banks along the upper reaches. Such a feast inevitably attracts other predators and scavengers and bears and Glaucous-winged Gulls vie with the Eagles in their enjoyment of the bonanza. Even here, however, Bald Eagles are far from pure scavengers. Birds will plunge down from a perch to grab living salmon as they struggle upstream as well as wrestle with spent and dying fish.

This association of Bald Eagles with fish has been cemented in the mind by many a wildlife movie, but also has a sound basis in fact. All of the eagles of the genus *Haliaeetus* are basically "fish-eagles." They are found throughout the world and most share the common feature of having white heads and tails. Most are capable fishermen, but are also opportunists, and

Bald Eagle
Haliaeetus leucocephalus

will readily turn to stranded fish and marine mammals – indeed any other substantial source of food. The Bald Eagle is probably the most adaptable of them all and is able to utilize a wide range of food sources.

Coastal dwelling Bald Eagles often take large numbers of seabirds and in some places this may form their main diet. They may fly low between the waves to surprise a group of auks, or plunge, falcon-like, out of the sky. Some birds have been seen grabbing seabirds in flight, while others have even been observed robbing a Peregrine of its prey, pirate-fashion. Fish caught in dives are generally about a pound in weight, but salmon dragged from shallow water may be several times that. Bald Eagles have also been recorded killing young sea otters, and even an Emperor Goose weighing over 6 pounds. Inland breeding Bald Eagles regularly take fish and wildfowl, but will also resort to the hills like a Golden Eagle and kill various ptarmigan species by a surprise quartering technique.

The Bald Eagle is purely a North American bird. It breeds from Alaska across Canada, from the Yukon and British Columbia to New Brunswick and Newfoundland. Though it is far less common in the east than the west. In the United States it has been eliminated over much of the eastern half of the country, though there are birds in the Appalachians as well as in Florida. In the west it breeds through the northern and eastern Rockies south almost to the Mexican border. Though only twelve hundred pairs are now found in the contiguous United States several thousand, perhaps as many as twenty thousand, move southward from Canada and Alaska to winter, particularly along the west coast where birds range as far south as Baja California. Birds that breed in Florida move northwards to winter, meeting up with Canadian birds moving south. This reverse migration may take Florida birds as far north as southern Canada by mid-summer, presumably in search of food.

Like most other large raptors, Bald Eagles start breeding early in the year, though inland Alaskan and northern Canadian birds cannot do so until the rivers and lakes are unfrozen. The nest is usually built in a tree and constructed of twigs and branches. Such nests are used over and over again and grow to enormous proportions as fresh material is added each season. In areas such as islands in the Bering Sea, where no trees are available, Bald Eagles will readily nest on cliffs and use

seaweed and other jetsam to build their nests. Inland and on coast alike, the nest lining consists of any old debris and rubbish they can find including, over the past twenty or thirty years, the inevitable polythene.

The two, occasionally three, white eggs are incubated thirty-four or thirty-five days mainly by the female, though with some assistance from the male. When she leaves the nest to feed the female covers the eggs with nesting material, a habit unique among eagles. As with other eagles it is unusual for more than one chick to survive, though this seems to be a result of competition for food rather than direct persecution by the older and stronger eaglet. They spend some seventy to seventy-seven days being fed and tended by the adults before they can fly and are dependent on their parents for several more weeks while they develop effective hunting techniques before becoming fully independent. The abundance of fish in Canadian rivers and lakes, however, ensures that few die at this time of the year. In the long days of summer adults seldom have to hunt for more than four hours a day. At first young birds are all brown with only an area of white at the base of the tail and on the wing linings. Gradually they become whiter on head and tail, though they are not fully adult until five years old. Young birds can be confused with adult Golden Eagles, but have a larger head and smaller tail giving them a slightly unbalanced "weight-forward" look.

Bald Eagles form communal roosts in winter while immatures continue to do so through the summer. They are not strictly gregarious, but often gather at suitable open water after being driven south by the winter freeze-up. At this time the outflows of large dams often keep water from freezing and several eagles may gather together at such sites. At the Chilkat River up to four thousand Eagles may congregate in the fall to feed on the late run of salmon. Later the river freezes up save for a stretch fed by hot springs. Here the Eagles gather to feed on dead salmon that may have been deep-frozen in the upper reaches several weeks before. Provided food is easily obtained,

young bald eagle exercising wings

the Eagles spend most of their time at a suitable perch and move only when forced to do so. Sometimes a bird will sit motionless for hours at a time.

In recent years Bald Eagles, along with so many other birds of prey, have suffered dramatic declines in numbers due to agricultural pesticides. These, especially DDT, build up in the fatty tissue of the adults and interfere seriously with their breeding. Thin eggshells are a typical symptom and these are impossible for the birds to incubate. A decline in breeding success has inevitably led to a decline in numbers. Unfortunately such poisons, which the birds ingest by way of their food, are remarkably persistent and will remain in the environment as a threat for many years to come. Otherwise the Bald Eagle is generally doing well, encouraged by the more enlightened attitude towards birds of prey that has been generated in recent years.

Bald Eagles
chasing Osprey

Ruffed Grouse

Ruffed Grouse

Female Spruce Grouse

The Ruffed Grouse is one of the sportsman's favorite birds throughout its range. In Canada hunters call it the "Birch Grouse," while in the northern United States it is known simply as the "Partridge" and in the southern States as the "Pheasant." Though placed on its own in the genus *Bonasa* it actually belongs to a small group of three closely related birds that between them cover most of the northern hemisphere. Formerly both the Hazel Grouse (*Tetrastes bonasia*) and Sewerzow's Grouse (*Tetrastes sewerzowi*) were also included in the genus *Bonasa*, but these even more closely related birds differ in various ways and have been split off from our own Ruffed Grouse. All three are birds of the northern forests and all bear a strong resemblance to the Turkey in having long, broad tail feathers that can be spread to form a fan.

The Ruffed Grouse is prized by sportsmen for the challenge it offers to the man with a gun. From a standing start it explodes into the air with a clattering of wings and disappears among the trees in a burst of acceleration that leaves the novice with a half-cocked gun and a look of surprise and disappointment. As it speeds away the Ruffed Grouse often puts trees and bushes between it and its pursuer in an apparently deliberate attempt to evade capture. However, once shot its flesh is said to taste quite delicious and it is much sought after as a table bird.

To sportsmen and birders alike the sound of a displaying cock is one of the most intriguing and evocative sounds of the northern forests in spring. This starts with slow dull thuds or thumps and rapidly accelerates into a whirring that may actually be painful to the ear if approached too closely. The whole performance lasts about 11 seconds and is repeated every few minutes. To many observers it has given the impression of the muffled sound of a distant car being started somewhere in the forest.

In fact the Ruffed Grouse is one of the very few birds – another that comes readily to mind is the Common Snipe – that is actually an instrumentalist rather than a vocalist. Careful stalking of the sound through the forest reveals the male strutting up and down on a fallen log. Its wings are drooped, its ruff of neck feathers spread and its tail erect like a cock Turkey. Then, lowering its tail, it slowly beings to beat its wings producing the rhythmic thudding that marks the beginning of its "song." The wings whirr faster and faster and the noise they create accelerates into the vibrant drumming. At the climax it is impossible to see either the wings move or distinguish between the sounds of the different beats, so swiftly are they produced. At the end of the performance the bird recommences his strutting up and down his drumming log. Ruffed Grouse come in two distinct color phases that live happily together. Grayish birds are most common in northern Canada while rufous birds predominate in the south. These differences are most obvious in the color of the tail. Additionally, a great many subspecies have been described including no fewer than nine from Canada alone. In this Ruffed Grouse are typical of a great many birds that are totally resident, being hatched and spending their lives in only a confined area of forest.

The male Ruffed Grouse is a mottled and barred, brown and buff bird marked by a small crest at the point of the crown. The upperparts have considerable areas of warm chestnut forming streaks on the back and bars across the wing. The large tail is grayish-brown to reddish-brown regularly barred with black. The tail tips show a broad black band bordered on both sides by narrow bands of white. These are extra-ordinarily beautiful feathers that are saved and taken home by anyone fortunate enough to find them. The underparts vary from pale cream to reddish-buff and are heavily barred with black. At the sides of the neck there is a smudgy patch of black. This is actually the ruff from which the Ruffed Grouse is named, for in display these feathers are spread to form a black collar completely encircling the neck. The hen is similar, but much less colorful in shades of gray, buff and brown. She also lacks the small red wattle of the male.

The Ruffed Grouse is found in the great belt of forest that occupies the northern half of North America. It is thus more common in Canada than anywhere else in the world. It

Ruffed Grouse
Bonasa umbellus

prefers open lightly forested areas to dense conifers and is, therefore, more generally associated with birch scrub. It is found among younger conifers and along the edges of older forests, though it will often use such forests in winter.

These are mainly vegetarian birds taking large quantities of berries, seeds, shoots and leaves throughout the year. Insects in their various forms as well as beetles and spiders make up just over a tenth of their food, though they are far more important in spring and summer and are the predominant food of the growing chicks. In winter, when snow covers the ground effectively hiding large quantities of food from the birds, Grouse often turn their attention to the leaves of laurel. Sometimes they consume so much laurel that people who have eaten such birds have suffered severe food poisoning. In spring the birds will occasionally turn their attention to the fruit buds of apple trees bringing them in sharp contact with the growers. Strangely, however, their pruning may actually help to produce a bumper crop of fruit in the fall.

Ruffed Grouse breed from central Alaska, through the Yukon to Hudson Bay and northwards to north-eastern Quebec. South of this line they extend to California in the west and beyond the Great Lakes to the eastern United States. They are resident throughout this huge area, but their numbers vary greatly from year to year. They reach a peak in population about every ten years.

The female creates the nest under cover of a fallen tree or among dense undergrowth. It consists of no more than a

foot
adapted
for snow

Blue Grouse

"deflating"

Ruffed
Grouse

Ruffed
Grouse

Spruce Grouse

The display of Woodland Grouse

simple depression in the ground lined with a few leaves and feathers. The nine to twelve eggs are buffy, sometimes lightly speckled with differing shades of brown, but often quite plain. Incubation, which starts when the clutch is complete, lasts for about twenty-four days and is performed by the female alone. Like other grouse she is a tight sitter and relies on her camouflaged plumage to protect herself and her nest. When finally approached too close she explodes into the air with a great beating of wings that startles the unsuspecting intruder.

As soon as they hatch the down-covered chicks leave the nest under the careful guidance of the female that teaches them to find food. If danger threatens the chicks crouch motionless on the ground at a shrill whining call from their mother. She meanwhile will produce a fluttering display over the ground as if injured in order to draw the attention of any would-be predator away from her brood. The chicks mature early and can fly when only half their adult size. They stay together and form coveys with other families through the following winter.

Ruffed Grouse display and drumming

Ruffed Grouse
on nest

Great Grey Owl hunting

Willow Ptarmigan

Willow Ptarmigan are one of the primary quarries of sportsmen wherever they occur. In North America they are confined to Canada and Alaska, but they are also found right across Northern Europe and Siberia to the Bering Sea. Throughout this huge circumpolar range they are resident, indeed the average Willow Ptarmigan will not move much more than a few miles throughout its life. Not surprisingly various subspecies have developed including ten distinct forms in Canada, though by far the most famous subspecies has developed in Britain and Ireland. Here the Willow Ptarmigan is known as the Red Grouse, a bird that lacks the white wings of the Willow Ptarmigan throughout the rest of its range and which was generally regarded as a separate species until some twenty years ago.

The Red Grouse is the keystone of one of the world's most status conscious sports 'Grouse shooting'. Every year on August 12th (the Glorious Twelfth) the highly managed and superbly keepered grouse moors echo to the sound of some of the most expensive shooting in the world. Earls, Dukes, Lords and plain everyday tycoons bang away at the season's crop of Grouse. The slaughter is incredible, but as the moors are managed to produce an artificially high population all is well and the Grouse population carefully maintained to produce a further shootable surplus the following year.

The more typical white-winged Willow Grouse, similar to our own Canadian birds, is a prime quarry throughout Scandinavia and indeed across the Russian parts of its Soviet range, though whether all comrades have equal access to the sport is not known. In Canada Willow Ptarmigan are found across the northern provinces beyond the tree line, extending southwards through the Rockies almost to the United States border.

The reasons for the species's popularity as a gamebird need little searching. Willow Ptarmigan generally prefer to keep to the ground and walk away from danger among the cover of heather and dwarf shrubs they inhabit. It is thus possible for the sportsman to walk well within gunshot range before the birds are pressed into flight. At this point they burst into the air with incredible acceleration before gliding away on bowed wings for a short distance. It needs a good shot to react quickly enough to down a "walked-up" bird. In Britain, and especially Scotland, the Red Grouse are "beaten" by a team of keepers so that they fly over the guns who are hidden in ambush. Shooting "beaten Grouse" is thus very much a social occasion and the "bags" are accordingly high. Young Grouse, in particular, make very good eating.

In summer Willow Ptarmigan are beautifully marked in shades of brown and rust forming a highly effective camouflage. The wings are white, but remain hidden until the bird flies. There is a prominent red comb above the eye that is much reduced in the generally paler and less rusty female. In winter the Willow Ptarmigan becomes pure white to hide itself among the snow that then covers its home. At this season it bears a strong resemblance to the Rock Ptarmigan

though males lack the black mark through the eye of that species. Females of both species are difficult to separate from each other and from male Willow Ptarmigan and the observer must rely on the larger size and strongly built bill of the present species.

Willow Ptarmigan are highly territorial. The male crows his *ko-ko-ko-ko-krr* calls early every morning from a prominent hillock in his otherwise bare domain. Females respond with a mewing call that then attracts the territorial male. Most males form a pair with a single female, but some manage to acquire two mates, while others that hold territories may have none at all. Every area of available habitat will be neatly divided up among the males, though it is those males that hold the most suitable territories at the centre that are most successful in attracting a mate.

The female constructs her nest within the male's territory. This consists of not much more than a depression in the ground lined with a few grasses and leaves. Between six and nine, most commonly seven or eight, eggs are laid, yellowish and heavily blotched and spotted with dark brown. They are

Willow Ptarmigan
Lagopus lagopus

incubated by the female for nineteen to twenty-five days, starting when the clutch is complete. She is a remarkably tight sitter and on at least one occasion a hen has been burnt to death rather than leave her eggs. The chicks all hatch within a few hours of each other and are covered in buff and black down that is an effective camouflage against predators. They leave the nest soon after hatching and are brooded by the female, though the male also joins in the task of caring for his brood. Though capable of flying after only twelve or thirteen days the chicks are not fully grown until thirty to thirty-five days. They become independent after about sixty days, but may be abandoned after forty-five days in poor years. At this time territorial boundaries are negated and all birds join into coveys that roam the moors together. Birds breed at one year old.

Willow Ptarmigan are mostly vegetarians throughout the year. Their diet consists of whatever is most abundant which, in Scotland, is mainly heather. In winter, when snow covers the ground vegetation, large amounts of birch and

Snowy Owl chasing Ptarmigan

willow catkins, buds and twigs are eaten. The Willow Ptarmigan is aptly named for this tree is certainly preferred food wherever it is available. In summer, when there is a wider variety of foods, the Willow Ptarmigan is much more catholic in its choice. It takes many insects and other invertebrates and for the chicks animate food forms a significant part of their daily intake. This does, however, decline rapidly with age and after 3 weeks is quite insignificant.

Breeding success varies greatly from year to year. By the fall the flocks are breaking up once again as males stake out and defend their territories. Non-territorial males and females maintain flocks throughout the winter and are joined by the territorial males during the afternoons. Gradually, as the winter progresses males spend less and less time with the flocks. Males that fail to obtain a territory usually die of starvation by being forced into marginal habitats. The flocks themselves feed in areas between territories in the mornings and in territories from which the owner is absent in the afternoons. Pairs generally form in early spring.

Rock Ptarmigan

Rock Ptarmigan
summer ♀

Ptarmigan
flight feather
black ribbed

The Rock Ptarmigan, though closely related and similar to the Willow Ptarmigan in appearance, is the Arctic replacement of that species. It is generally found to the north of the Willow Ptarmigan or, where the two overlap, occurs at higher altitudes. In Canada it is thus a tundra bird occurring only in the Yukon, the Northwest Territories, northern Quebec and Newfoundland, although it extends as far as southern British Columbia in the Rockies. It is also found in the archepelago as far north as open land exists, including northern Ellesmere Island, one of the most severe habitats in the world. Elsewhere it occurs around the coasts of Greenland, Iceland, on the highest mountains of Scotland and Scandinavia and right across northern Siberia. It is, however, also found in the mountains of central Asia, in the Alps and reaches its farthest south in the Pyrennees.

In general it is resident with only local movements to lower altitudes. However, northernmost Canadian birds do leave their hostile environment and move southwards to milder climes sometimes as far as the St Lawrence, well to the south of their breeding range. One bird ringed in Greenland was recovered six hundred and twenty-five miles to the south and there is indirect evidence of birds leaving that frozen land and making the overseas flight to Iceland. Such long distance movements are unusual among gamebirds, but show a close similarity to the eruptive behaviour of other arctic breeding species like lemmings and Snowy Owls.

In general Ptarmigan stay at or near their breeding grounds. They are confiding birds relying heavily on their excellent camouflage to protect them from predators. As a result they are easily overlooked and many a birder has suddenly found himself walking among a flock of these birds where he had seen none only a few moments before. Their delicate colours are a mixture of grays, buffs and white woven together in a highly cryptic fashion. In summer they are mostly gray, and in winter almost entirely white, except for a black mark connecting bill and eye in the male. Both sexes retain white

Rock Ptarmigan

Lagopus mutus

wings throughout the year, just like the Willow Ptarmigan. Rock Ptarmigan generally avoid areas with any substantial growth of vegetation and find their food among the lichens and mosses of stony ground. They feed mostly on dwarf plants such as willow and heather and seldom take much animate food. In winter they will use their feathered feet to excavate snow and gain access to plants beneath. They show a preference for willow where the Willow Ptarmigan does not exist as, for instance, in Iceland, but in Alaska, where both species can be found, the Rock Ptarmigan takes birch even though willow is available. In this way competition between these two closely related species is avoided. Only young chicks, less than a week old, take any quantity of insect food.

In winter Ptarmigan form into flocks which may number a hundred or more birds. In Canada, though not elsewhere, such flocks tend to be of a single sex, with the females occupying more sheltered lower and southerly areas, while the males are found both higher and further north in more severe conditions. In the northernmost parts of the range, where the summer is shortest, flocks remain together till late in the spring. Then, quite suddenly, they break up. Males establish territories, display, pair and mate in the briefest possible time. Most Rock Ptarmigan form monogamous partnerships, though in more northern territories males often mate with two or three females. In Iceland the birds are promiscuous with females only associating with males

during mating. It has been suggested that this is because of higher predation of the territorial males by Gyrfalcons, though this bird is decidedly rare there.

Despite its scientific name, *Lagopus mutus*, the Rock Ptarmigan is far from silent. It utters a series of extraordinary calls that are very difficult to transcribe either in words or phrases. The calls of the male have been likened to the series of clicks created by running a stick along a slatted wooden fence.

The nest consists of a natural hollow lined with twigs, leaves, grasses and a few breast feathers. It is generally sheltered by a rock or small bush, though it is occasionally placed on open ground. Both sexes participate in nest building and, if time permits, several alternatives are constructed before one is finally chosen. The male starts creating scrapes up to two weeks before egg laying, but the female joins in only when egg laying is imminent. The five to eight, usually six or seven, rich cinnamon eggs are blotched and spotted with brown, though they fade to buff during incubation. They are laid at one or two day intervals and are covered with nest lining until the clutch is complete. The twenty-one to twenty-three days of incubation are performed by the female alone starting with the last or second to last egg. Meanwhile the

Rock Ptarmigan in winter plumage

male departs to gather in small flocks to molt, though in some parts of its range the male accompanies the female when she leaves the nest to feed. In these areas the male may even help with caring for the chicks, though in Canada this is seldom so.

The chicks, which are self-feeding are capable of flying when only ten to fifteen days old, though they do not become independent until ten or even twelve weeks. Throughout this period they are guarded by the female that, like so many other gamebirds has a well developed distraction display to lure predators away from her brood. The birds are capable of breeding at one year old.

At the end of the breeding season coveys are formed that are generally small, but which may build up to several hundred birds. Gradually the grays and browns of summer are lost and an increasing proportion of the plumage is white. Though a pure white bird on a gray landscape would be remarkably conspicuous, as indeed would a gray bird on a snowy white background, the patchy mixture of gray and white has the effect of breaking up the bird's outline and keeping it hidden. Birds may even select the areas they use according to the state of their plumage: snowfields when white and rocky areas when gray.

During the winter birds will seek shelter by crouching in small hollows, behind hummocks or even in human footprints. In exceptional circumstances the Rock Ptarmigan will excavate a hole in the snow so that only its head remains visible.

Greater Prairie Chicken

The Greater Prairie Chicken is a typical grouse of open prairie that was once found throughout the grasslands east of the Rockies. Though its population, like that of the Ruffed Grouse, varies season by season reaching a peak about every ten years, it has declined catastrophically during the present century. A variety of causes are undoubtedly involved.

Shooting certainly played a major part in its decline and may still contribute to its ultimate demise. Conservation is not aided by the fact that the bird is often confused with the much more widespread and numerous Sharp-tailed Grouse. Today shooting may be an important factor hindering efforts to save the Prairie Chicken, but it could hardly be the major factor. Prairie fires have also played a part in the decline, especially those that occur in the breeding season. However, the extension of agriculture to what were once open grasslands together with a subsequent high level of mechanization is undoubtedly the most significant cause of all. In Canada this is now a very rare bird indeed, and its situation is far from secure south of the border. In Alberta it was present in the 1890s, but then declined rapidly. The last record was of one near Medicine Hat in 1940. In Saskatchewan it was quite common until the 1920s, but then declined so rapidly that only two were seen in 1959 and one in 1960. A similar story can be told of Manitoba. Only in Ontario does the Greater Prairie Chicken seem to still be seen regularly and even there its history is a chequered one. It bred until about the end of last century and then disappeared. It was found again in 1925 on St Joseph's Island spreading to Manitoulin Island in 1938. It still exists there, but regularly hybridizes with Sharp-tailed Grouse. It can, therefore, be only a matter of time before this super bird disappears from Canada altogether.

South of the border the situation is critical. The eastern subspecies known as the Heath Hen was already exterminated by 1926. In Texas the local subspecies known as

Greater Prairie Chicken
display postures

Attwater's Prairie Chicken was down to seven hundred and fifty birds twenty years ago and like the other subspecies was awarded a place in the Red Data Book which details birds in danger of extinction. Elsewhere there are pockets of birds in South Dakota, Nebraska, Kansas and Oklahoma, but all are endangered and only the conservation of natural grasslands seems likely to prevent their ultimate extinction. In Illinois there are a hundred or so in captivity where they seem to breed quite well, so there is always hope of re-introductions provided that sufficient space can be set aside within the confines of refuges and free of agriculture.

The Greater Prairie Chicken is a heavily barred buff and brown bird marked by a short tail, black and buff wings and a small tuft of feathers that hang from the sides of the neck. These cover orange yellow air sacs that are inflated in display.

72

Greater Prairie Chicken
Typanuchus cupido

Sharp-tailed
Grouse

Burrowing
Owl

During the spring males gather at special lekking grounds where they perform elaborate displays making much use of their tails, wings and inflatable neck sacs. These sacs are part of the bird's vocal equipment and are used in producing a hollow booming call that has been likened to the sound produced by blowing across the top of an empty bottle. Having called, the bird then cackles, jumps in the air, twists around and, tail and wings spread, charges its neighbors. Sometimes these charging rushes lead to actual fighting.

Having visited the lek and mated with the male of her choice, the female builds her nest in a hollow in the ground lined with grass among bushes or tall grass. It is by no means easy to find. The eleven or twelve eggs, occasionally more, are pale olive spotted with light brown. Incubation, by the female alone, lasts twenty-three to twenty-four days and the down covered chicks leave the nest soon after hatching. They can feed themselves straight away and take a variety of insects as well as much plant material. The female tends and cares for them until they reach independence.

Prairie Chicken are naturally adapted to feeding on the seeds, shoots and leaves of grassland, though they also take berries. They do, however, consume large quantities of grasshoppers and other insects and are generally regarded as beneficial to agriculture. It is a pity that bird and man cannot co-exist.

Though Sharp-tailed Grouse are easily confused by the layman, no birder need ever find the two difficult to separate. The Prairie chicken has barred not spotted underparts, and a shorter dark, not white, tail. Compared to the Ruffed Grouse its short tail lacking a black band is usually quite obvious.

The Lesser Prairie Chicken (*Tympanuchus pallidicinctus*) is often regarded as a further subspecies of the Greater Prairie Chicken, though the official view is that it is a distinct species. It occurs only in the south-western United States in New Mexico, Colorado, Kansas, Oklahoma and Texas and is rapidly declining. Its population seems to vary but it is doubtful if more than fifty thousand birds remain, probably many fewer.

Sage Grouse

As its name implies, the Sage Grouse is a bird that is almost totally confined to areas where sage brush dominates the landscape, areas which have become few and far between in this country. Today it is found only in south-eastern Alberta between Wildhorse and Manyberries and in south-western Saskatchewan between Cypress Hills and Wood Mountain. In each case the range extends across the United States boundary into the rolling sage brush country to the south where this grouse finds its natural home. It is unknown elsewhere in the world. It also used to breed around Osoyoos Lake in southern British Columbia, but has now been exterminated there. These latter birds belonged to a separate subspecies that still exists across the border.

Throughout its range Sage Grouse have proved a favorite target for sportsmen and have been much reduced in numbers. This is, at first sight, somewhat surprising since birds that have fed on sage apparently make poor eating and have a strangely bitter taste. Young birds that have fed on grasshoppers and other insects are more palatable. Yet this has not deterred the hunters that find in the species great sporting character. Like other grouse and ptarmigan they are mainly ground-dwelling birds that prefer to walk away from danger and rely on their camouflage to protect them from predators. As a result they are easily "walked up." When finally put to flight they explode with a clatter of wings that is quite startling, before flying away swiftly and strongly. There is thus considerable skill involved in "bagging" Sage Grouse which, naturally enough, makes them the preserve of the good shot rather than the beginner.

So effective is their camouflage that there are many stories of people standing within a yard or two of a sitting hen for some time before noticing her presence. Indeed, such stories are so numerous that there must be many more occasions when the sitting bird is not noticed and the intruder walks away unknowingly. Both sexes are mottled buff and brown and merge with the dry landscape they inhabit, but these are far

Sage Grouse
Centrocercus urophasianus

from small birds. A male may measure up to twenty-nine inches and a female up to twenty-three inches. The male is larger and has a longish pointed tail, a pale breast, a bold pattern of black and white on the head and breast, and a small yellow comb over the eye. The female lacks these markings, but like her mate, has a black belly.

Sage Grouse were first discovered by Clark and Lewis in their great exploration of the west between 1804 and 1806. They called the birds "cock of the plains," but a proper scientific description was not made until 1827 when the distinguished ornithologist Bonaparte (he of "Bonaparte's Gull" etc) named the bird. At that time the Sage Grouse was undoubtedly more numerous than it is today, though it is doubtful if it enjoyed a much wider range.

These Grouse are more or less confined to those areas where sage grows profusely – the home of the American cowboy film. Sage is its primary food and the bird seldom ventures very far from it. It regularly flights to gullies and rivers to drink and roost among trees and will also seek shade from intense heat. In summer it regularly feeds on wild peas of various species, taking buds, leaves and seed pods as available. In some areas it takes large amounts of blossom and in others will even make commuting flights of several miles to take wheat. Despite this apparent adaptability, the bird is still dependent on sage and is very appropriately named.

Though the male Sage Grouse is a well camouflaged, one could almost say drab, bird it performs a particularly distinctive display designed to make it as conspicuous as possible. Well before dawn males flight to their communal lek, an area of ground virtually devoid of vegetation. Here, each bird establishes a tiny area which it defends against other males. Each spreads its tail into a Turkey-like fan, save that each of the twenty feathers is sharply pointed. The wings are brought forward and spread. The chest is pumped up and the white chest feathers spread and puff up to reveal two large orange-yellow air sacs. At the height of its display the cock bird seems to have difficulty even in seeing forward over his chest. Strutting forward the wings and breast feathers produce a swishing noise while the air sacs are pumped up until they seem ready to burst. A loud "plop" is then produced that can be heard up to a quarter of a mile away. The process is then repeated over and over again. With anything up to a

Sage
Grouse
display

hundred birds present at a single display ground the noise serves to draw females from a considerable distance. As with so many lek-based displays it is the males at the centre that seem to be most attractive and mate with the largest number of females.

Once mated the female Sage Grouse departs to rear her brood without help from her mate. She constructs the nest, which is no more than a depression in the ground lined with a few grasses, usually beneath a sage bush. The seven to nine eggs vary from olive-buff to greenish-white spotted with brown. Incubation lasts for about twenty two days and the female, as we have noted, is a very tight sitter. The chicks, like other young gamebirds, leave the nest soon after hatching and are self-feeding. They are cared for and brooded by the female. The chicks take large quantities of grasshoppers, ants, moths and other animate food. As they grow the fall brings a bountiful crop of berries and seeds.

Sage Grouse
on nest ♀♀

Sage Grouse
taking
flight

Sage Grouse ♀

young Sage Grouse

Bobwhite

The Bobwhite, or Bobwhite Quail as it is often known, is one of those birds that has been named from its distinctive call. Its whistled *bob-bob-white* is a common sound of open country throughout the United States east of the Rockies, but one that is unfortunately only rarely heard in Canada. Strangely, the northern limits of this attractive little bird co-incide almost exactly with our southern border and the Bobwhite is restricted, as a Canadian bird, to the area of southern Ontario that extends southwards between Lakes Huron, Erie and Ontario. Here, as elsewhere in its range, it is resident in scrub and open forest adjacent to grassland, though it also frequents grain and corn fields especially if neglected and overgrown with weeds.

In Ontario it extends northwards to Brant, Middlesex, Oxford and Lincoln counties. As with so many popular gamebirds, the Bobwhite has been introduced to various other areas where it is not naturally found. Mostly such introductions have failed, though the birds still manage to survive at Huntingdon in south-western British Columbia as well as across the border in the adjacent United States. Elsewhere several attempts have been made to introduce Bobwhites as gamebirds notably in England where twenty attempts have been made since 1813. Some have bred for a few years but none have established themselves. In France no less than sixty-five thousand birds have been released with

'heads down'

better results, probably because the brush-covered habitat the birds prefer is more abundant in that country. They now breed ferally in at least eleven distinct areas of the south and centre of the country, though they are not as yet admitted to the official list of French birds.

The Bobwhite is a finely marked little bird some nine or ten inches long. Both sexes are brown above. The breast and belly are heavily barred with black, while the flanks show a regular pattern of large brown arrows pointing toward the tail. The male has a white head marked by a dark brown cap and a bold black line extending through the eye to the throat where it forms a prominent breast band. In the female this pattern is less bold and contrasting in shades of buff and brown. The overall impression is of a small partridge rather than of a quail, such as the California Quail, which occurs west of the Rockies.

Bobwhite are gregarious in winter forming small coveys up to 30 strong. Larger coveys, up to a hundred birds, are occasionally found, but are decidedly unusual. When disturbed the covey bursts into the air offering a chance to only the fastest of guns. In spring these flocks break up as males fight among themselves for a mate. Once pairs have been formed they move away from the flock to establish their territory which the male defends and delimits by repeated

a covey sleeping

slipping through grass

bouts of calling. The *bob-bob-white* call, which is reiterated for five minutes at a time, is uttered from a high perch such as the top of a bush or a fence post. It is a clearly whistled call that terminates with a ringing note.

Unusually among gamebirds, the male Bobwhite takes a fair share of the nesting duties. The nest itself consists of a hollow, usually well hidden beneath a tussock of grass, lined with grasses and leaves. The clutch is normally twelve to fourteen creamy-colored eggs, though up to sixteen have been counted in a single nest. In Canada these are laid in May, though further south they may be laid at the end of April. Incubation commences when the clutch is complete and lasts for twenty-three or twenty-four days. This duty is shared between members of the pair and the sitting bird will often pull surrounding vegetation over itself as an aid to camouflage. Whether such behavior is more prevalent among the more boldly marked, and thus more conspicuous males has not been properly investigated.

The chicks hatch out within a few hours of each other and are covered in brown and white down that effectively hides them from predators. They leave the nest within a day of hatching

Male and Female Bobwhite

Bobwhite
Colinus virginianus

and are able to feed themselves straight away. Both parents tend and guard the brood and have a well developed distraction display to draw predators away from their young. This consists of scurrying over the ground as if injured – a "broken-wing" display similar to that found in several species of shorebirds. Like so many other gamebirds young Bobwhites can fly long before they are fully grown. Indeed their wing feathers start to appear within a day or so of hatching and the young birds can be airborne within a week. Such a strategy is of great value to what is essentially a ground-dwelling bird and offers an alternative to the crouch-and-hide method of avoiding predators.

86

During the summer months Bobwhite take large quantities of insects, including many species that are harmful to agriculture. In spring buds and shoots may be important, though generally the birds rely on seeds of a wide variety of plant species as their staple diet throughout the year. With the coming of fall families of Bobwhites join together to form their winter coveys once more. Together they roam the countryside in search of food, though they seldom travel very far from their birthplace. At this time they coexist quite happily with none of the fighting and jealousies of spring and summer. The birds roost together on the ground forming a circle in which each individual faces outwards. In hard weather the circle is tightened with individual birds pressed tightly together for warmth.

For a long while it was a matter of debate as to whether young Bobwhites learned this roosting method from their parents or other adults, or whether it was purely instinctive. That it was the latter was proved when week old chicks hatched by a broody Bantam adopted the circular roost without ever seeing an adult. Such an arrangement does have considerable advantages, for not only does it maintain body heat by clustering tightly together, but in an emergency each bird can fly directly away without hinderance or collision with its fellows.

The Bobwhite is an attractive bird that is popular with both sportsmen and farmers. It is a great pity that its distinctive whistled call is not a more familiar sound of the Canadian countryside.

California Quail

Mountain Quail

The California Quail is one of a group of similar quail of essentially western distribution that between them occupy the whole of the western United States and extend southwards to well below the Mexican border. Their closest relative is Gambel's Quail which was distinguished only as recently as 1841 by the eminent American ornithologist Dr William Gambel. While the California Quail is common in the well vegetated parts west of the main Rocky Mountain chain, Gambel's Quail is found in the more arid interior and south. Indeed, the two species not only bear a strong resemblance to one another, but actually overlap in range only in a tiny area of south-eastern California. Such lack of overlap indicates both a common ancestor and a fairly recent origin, in evolutionary terms at least. Species evolve in geographical isolation, but once distinct are then able to coexist side by side and occupy the same range. It is interesting that in the small area of overlap between the California and Gambel's Quail along the western edges of the Mojave and Colorado deserts, the two interbreed quite freely and hybrids survive quite well.

The male California Quail is grayish-brown above. The breast is gray and the belly a scaly pattern of buff and brown produced by brown edges to the buffy feathers. The flanks are brown, boldly streaked with creamy-white and the nape is heavily barred gray and brown. By far the most noticeable feature, however, is the head pattern. The crown is chestnut bordered by a white coronal ring. The face is black bordered and enclosed by white, while a small comma-shaped tuft of feathers extends from the crown in an erectile crest that curves forward over the bill. The female also has a crest, but is otherwise much duller than her mate in shades of brown with streaking and barring in cream. She completely lacks the bold face pattern of the male.

Gambel's Quail is virtually identical except that in both sexes the belly is a creamy-white instead of a scaly browny-buff and the male has a black belly patch. The male California Quail

California Quail
Lophortyx californicus

also has a pale yellowish forehead that is a surprisingly good identification mark in the field.

While Gambel's Quail is a desert bird, the California Quail is found in areas with a greater cover of vegetation. It frequents areas of scrub with low trees broken by more open areas of grass. Though much of its original habitat has been destroyed it has adapted well to man-made environments and is frequently encountered around buildings, farms, gardens and even city parks, where it is definitely on the increase.

Its natural range extends from southern Oregon and western Nevada through California to the Mexican border and throughout the Baja peninsular. It has, however, been successfully introduced to south-western British Columbia where it finds its only Canadian home. It is now well established around Victoria and Comax in the southern half of Vancouver Island, around Vancouver itself and in the Okanagan Valley, around Keremos and along Cache Creek. These northern introductions have effectively increased its range from the Canadian border to Mexico and made it the most successful of all the western Quail. Elsewhere it has been introduced to large areas of the west including Washington, Northern Oregon, Idaho, Colorado and Utah. It has even been transported overseas and now seems well established in Hawaii.

During most of the year California Quail are found in coveys up to thirty strong. They feed together, spending most of their time on the ground pecking at the leaves and buds that form the main element of their diet. They also take berries in season, but only very small quantities of insect and other animate food. Quite often the feeding flock is guarded by a single, watchful bird perched in an adjacent tree. If danger threatens, the guard utters a high-pitched chattering note of alarm that sends the whole flock scurrying for cover. Because the birds generally run rather than fly from danger they are not regarded as a good gamebird and are seldom shot. This may, in part, account for their tameness in occupying the parks and gardens of built-up areas where they will even gather at bird feeding stations.

In spring the flocks break up and males establish territories. They call frequently at this time uttering a loud *kurr* note that is quite distinct from their more regular call. The latter

a small covey

consists of three slightly slurred notes of which the middle is the loudest and highest. It has been variously rendered as *chicag-o*, *where-are-you*, *you-go-way*, and *wook-kook-ah*. These calls are most frequently heard at dawn, though dusk often produces another bout of calling.

Once a territory has been established the pair settle down to breed in May. The nest is a hollow in the ground lined with grass; roots and leaves, hidden beneath a bush or among shrubs. The ten to eighteen eggs vary from creamy-white to a warm buff and are marked with blotches and spots of brown and purple. The normal clutch is about twelve, and some larger clutches may be the result of more than one female laying in the same nest. The chicks leave the nest soon after hatching and, like so many other gamebirds, are highly precocious.

Being sedentary, a number of distinct subspecies has been described from various parts of its range. It is unfortunate that the birds that have been introduced to British Columbia come from various stocks and thus cannot be ascribed to a particular race.

Ring-necked Pheasant

The Pheasant is, without question, the world's most popular gamebird. A native of Asia, it has been introduced over large areas of Europe and North America, to New Zealand, and even to south-eastern Australia. Yet, strange as it may seem, the origins of its introduction to Europe pre-date the development of the shotgun by at least sixteen hundred years. It is said that the Romans first brought the Pheasant to Europe, but its introduction may well pre-date their empire.

At first such introductions were probably for ornamentation or possibly for food and the birds remained somewhat scarce. Then, in the nineteenth century, the English developed the sport of shooting with the by then perfected shotgun – a weapon that has changed little since the early part of that century. Suddenly Pheasants were in great demand and the new occupation of gamekeeper was developed to ensure that the gentry had more than sufficient Pheasants to indulge their sport. Pheasants were reared, copses were planted for cover and all enemies, as well as suspected enemies, were labelled vermin and exterminated. Though this led to a boom in the number of Pheasants it had disastrous effects on birds of prey.

The sport was highly organized and huge "bags" were made by the "driven" technique, in which a team of "beaters" rounds up the local Pheasant population and drives them over a string of well-positioned waiting guns. This is still the most popular form of shooting in the British Isles, though one that is becoming increasingly expensive. Elsewhere Pheasants are "walked up" by individual or groups of guns and shot as they are flushed. Whichever method is used the Pheasant has proved the ideal gamebird – good shooting and excellent eating.

Pheasants are found naturally from the shores of the Caspian Sea eastwards across central Asia to Korea and China. At first the birds introduced to Europe were, understandably, from

Ring-necked Pheasant
Phasianus colchicus

the alert head of the Cock Pheasant

the western part of this huge range. Later travelers brought birds from further east. Today no less than 31 distinct subspecies are recognized and a considerable number of these have been transported around the world to be introduced alongside existing stocks. The result is that introduced birds of various subspecies have interbred freely and show the character of a variety of different forms. Most common are the Chinese Ring-necked, the Black-necked and the Mongolian, but plumages vary from buff-brown to black. Many have a white ring around the neck, but others do not. Females vary from gray-buff to a rich chestnut.

Just when the Pheasant was introduced to Canada remains uncertain. Today they can be found from Queen Charlotte and Vancouver Islands, southern British Columbia and through the prairies of Alberta to Saskatchewan and south-western Manitoba. They are also well established in southern Ontario and along the St Lawrence River to New Brunswick and Nova Scotia. As elsewhere the various subspecies have been thoroughly mixed to provide a wide variety of different plumages.

Typically the cock Pheasant has a rich chestnut-red body barred with black, paler grayish wings, and an exceptionally long gray and black banded tail. The head and neck are dark bottle-green, with a large red wattle around the eye and the hint of a crest. The green head and chestnut body are separated by a clear white neck ring, from which the bird is named. The female is much more soberly clad in buffs and browns, being darker and more heavily barred above and paler below. In this she bears some resemblance to female ptarmigan, but is easily separated by a long pointed tail some two-thirds the length of the male's.

These birds are typical of the Far Eastern forms of the Pheasant, whereas western birds are generally darker and lack the white neck ring. These too can be found in Canada as can birds with golden rather than gray wings, blue rather than chestnut rumps, golden rather than rufous backs and even pinkish tails. A melanistic mutant has a dark bottle-green body and bears a strong resemblance to the Japanese Pheasant, which is actually a quite separate species that has also been introduced in various parts of the world.
Although Pheasants are frequently associated with marshes in their native range they have adapted well to agricultural

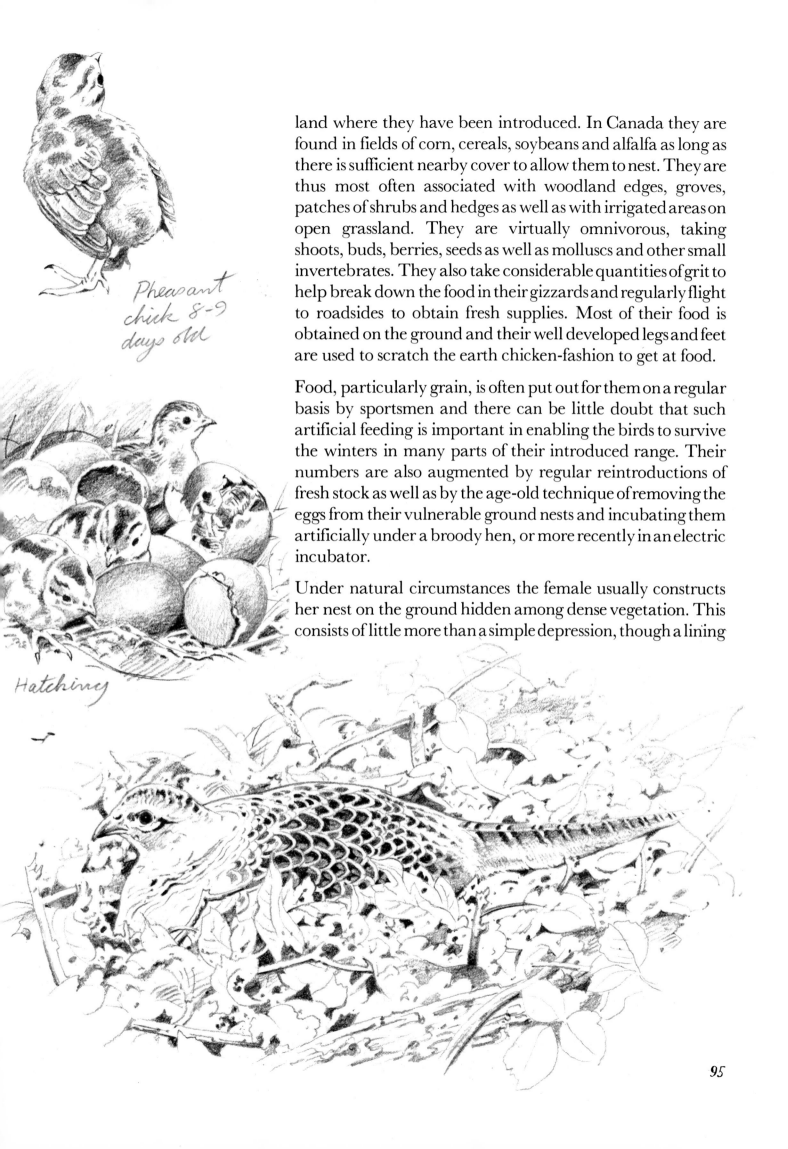

Pheasant chick 8-9 days old

Hatching

land where they have been introduced. In Canada they are found in fields of corn, cereals, soybeans and alfalfa as long as there is sufficient nearby cover to allow them to nest. They are thus most often associated with woodland edges, groves, patches of shrubs and hedges as well as with irrigated areas on open grassland. They are virtually omnivorous, taking shoots, buds, berries, seeds as well as molluscs and other small invertebrates. They also take considerable quantities of grit to help break down the food in their gizzards and regularly flight to roadsides to obtain fresh supplies. Most of their food is obtained on the ground and their well developed legs and feet are used to scratch the earth chicken-fashion to get at food.

Food, particularly grain, is often put out for them on a regular basis by sportsmen and there can be little doubt that such artificial feeding is important in enabling the birds to survive the winters in many parts of their introduced range. Their numbers are also augmented by regular reintroductions of fresh stock as well as by the age-old technique of removing the eggs from their vulnerable ground nests and incubating them artificially under a broody hen, or more recently in an electric incubator.

Under natural circumstances the female usually constructs her nest on the ground hidden among dense vegetation. This consists of little more than a simple depression, though a lining

of available material may be added. The eggs are smooth, glossy and mostly unmarked olive-brown. They are laid regularly at twenty-four hour intervals and generally number from eight to fifteen. Larger clutches, up to twenty-three eggs, are invariably the result of two hens laying in a single nest. If the eggs are lost, up to two relayings may be achieved. The female performs the twenty-three to twenty-eight days of incubation alone, starting only when the clutch is complete. The down covered chicks leave the nest as soon as they hatch and can feed themselves from the start. They are cared for by the female. Though males usually play no part in rearing their young this may well be due to the fact that males are more heavily shot than females. This actually reduces the number of males available in the population as mates, whereas in the wild there may well be a surplus of males. In more natural conditions males have been noted taking a share of incubation, despite their bright colors, and in some areas actually care for their brood for longer periods than the female.

Though they take seventy to eighty days to reach independence, the chicks are capable of flying when only twelve days old. About forty per cent of nests fail to produce young and over half of the failures are due to predators.

Clearly the Pheasant's ability to lay again following clutch loss is an important factor in the species's survival. In its native range there is evidence of some decline in numbers though, like other gamebirds, populations do vary considerably from year to year. Even where they are not heavily hunted, life expectancy is very short with less than one in five birds surviving their first year. Once past their first birthday Pheasants stand an even chance of living a further year. If these birds were to fall from favor as the primary hunting quarry their numbers would undoubtedly decline quite quickly leading to at least local extirpation.

The crowing call of the cock Pheasant is one of the characteristic sounds of the countryside in many parts of Canada. The loud *co-cock* can be heard at considerable distances and is often answered by an adjacent rival male. Indeed, where males are thick on the ground a more or less continuous crowing may occupy the first few hours after dawn. The male selects a prominent low perch and then calls regularly from it. Each call is followed by a series of wing beats that may be heard at close range. During courtship the male makes much of its boldly colored plumage and especially of the ear tufts, which are erected, and the facial wattles that are puffed up and swollen. Wings and tail are spread as the female is courted prior to mating.

Though Pheasants will burst into the air with a great beating of wings when disturbed they seldom fly very far. Indeed, once height has been gained they generally glide away at speed slowly losing height. Because they are incapable of sustained flight Pheasants tend to avoid large stretches of open water and the record distance flown by one of these birds is about four miles across a lake. There have, however, been several instances of Pheasants drowning, exhausted by attempting shorter flights over water.

Gray Partridge

If the Pheasant is the primary hunting target in woodland and copses, then the Gray Partridge is the number one quarry in open fields and heaths. First introduced to Canada for its sporting qualities, it can now be found in many southern areas of the country. It is well established and self supporting though reintroductions, especially in marginal habitats, are more or less continuously taking place. The birds suffer considerably in hard weather and large numbers may then die. At such times they may appear around farmsteads searching for snow free ground and grain spillages, especially where domestic animals are present. This may make them appear quite tame, though in fact it is sheer hunger that brings them into such close contact with man. That the Gray Partridge manages to survive so well in Canada is due to its high rate of recovery from winter disasters by virtue of a very high reproductive rate.

The bird is a native of Europe and west central Asia. It extends from Britain and France northwards to Finland and eastwards across Russia. In the south it is found in Italy, Bulgaria and in central Turkey, but is absent from most of the Mediterranean where it is replaced by the various species of "red-legged" partridges of the genus *Alectoris*. These birds prefer drier ground and, where they have been introduced in England, are dominant in the eastern and drier parts of the country. Indeed, they may have dispossessed Gray Partridge in these parts. In Canada the only representative of this genus is the Chukar which was introduced into southern British Columbia in 1950 and now seems to be doing well. More recent introductions in Saskatchewan may or may not prove successful. It will be interesting to see how well this native of the Middle East fares if and when its range overlaps with the better established Gray.

At present Gray Partridges inhabit southern British Columbia including southern Vancouver Island. They range northwards to central Alberta and central Saskatchewan and into the south-western quarter of Manitoba. In Ontario they are found in the south and east and there is a quite separate

Gray Partridge
Perdix perdix

population in New Brunswick and Nova Scotia. Throughout this vast area they are, however, more local than a glance at the map would indicate and it is possible to travel many miles without so much as a glimpse of this attractive bird.

Gray Partridges are brown above, mottled with buff and streaked with cream to form a highly effective camouflage when they crouch among ploughed fields. The head is a pale orange and the breast pale gray-blue. The underparts are creamy barred with chestnut on the flanks and with a bold horseshoe-shaped chestnut mark on the belly. The female is similar to the male, but paler and with only a small chestnut smudge on the belly. In flight birds of both sexes show bright rust-red corners to the tail, quite unlike any of our native gamebirds, though this feature is shared with the "red-legged" partridges including the Chukar. Juvenile Gray Partridges are somewhat nondescript and confusing being a warm creamy buff above and below with boldly barred brown and cream wings. In all plumages the legs and feet, as well as the bill, are grayish-black.

Partridges are gregarious birds spending most of their lives in small flocks known as coveys. Mostly these consist of between five and fifteen birds, but coveys up to twenty-five strong are quite frequent and occasionally groups will join together to form larger flocks on a temporary basis. Mostly these flocks consist of a core of a single family, plus a few individual adults that have failed to rear a family of their own. Sometimes two or more families will join together and occasionally a flock will consist entirely of adults. This, however, is the result of a disastrous breeding season and such groupings are seldom very large.

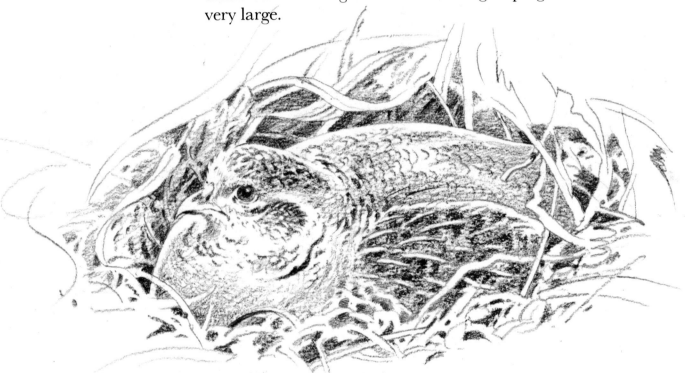

Each covey maintains its own communal territory around it. This territory is far from fixed, however, consisting of an area that changes as the flock moves about. In general this mobile territory has a limit of several hundred yards within which no other flock may or will encroach. If conditions are hard with snow covering the ground the birds become more tolerant and in exceptional freezing conditions coveys will feed alongside each other without aggression.

In the spring pairing within the covey takes place only between established couples. For although there is a certain amount of flirtation and unfaithfulness at the beginning of the season, the vast majority of Gray Partridges will breed with their established mate season after season as long as they both survive. Young birds breeding for the first time leave the flocks to establish territories by themselves and thus attract mates from outside their original family group. This is essential to prevent incestuous inbreeding. Sometimes young males will fight to defend their territory, though Gray Partridges are far from being male dominated. There are many instances of female dominance and even of one female killing another to gain the attentions of a particular male. Though the female is less brightly colored, she is not camouflaged like the females of so many other gamebirds.

The nest is built by the female and consists of a depression in the ground lined with whatever materials are within reach. The eggs are glossy olive-brown and number between ten and twenty. Clutches up to twenty-nine have been recorded and, though usually regarded as the work of two females, there are certainly records of a single hen laying up to twenty-four eggs. Such large clutches provide a fine insurance not only on an individual pair basis, but also in enabling the species to recover quickly after a disastrous winter.

Gray Partridge

Chukar
Red-legged Partridge

Though only one brood is reared, lost clutches will be quickly replaced, though normally with a smaller clutch than the original. Eggs are laid at intervals of about 1½ days and during the lengthy laying period the nest is covered with vegetation in the female's absence. Incubation begins with the last egg and is performed by the female alone for the twenty-three to twenty-five days before hatching. The male takes no part in this chore, but may well be present when the chicks hatch. The down-covered youngsters leave the nest soon after hatching and though tended by both adults are capable of feeding themselves. They can fly at fifteen days but do not achieve adult weight until they are three months old.

Eggs and chicks are prone to predators, but the main factor in successful breeding is the abundance of insect food for the young. Modern pesticides have successfully reduced the insect population of cereal crops in particular and, as a result, large numbers of Partridge chicks die of starvation. In several parts of their range there has been a serious decline in the number of these birds attributable to such modern agricultural practices. Yet it is difficult to persuade crop-conscious farmers to abandon spraying and leave pest control to the birds.

Common Snipe

The drumming of Snipe is a common sound of spring virtually throughout Canada. Rising high in the air the bird half-closes its wings and dives headlong toward the ground. In doing so the wind vibrates through the two specially stiffened outer tail feathers producing a loud bleating that can be heard at considerable distances. After one dive the Snipe climbs upwards once more to repeat its diving performance over and over again in a circle around its territory. It is thus one of the very few bird instrumentalists of which the woodpeckers come the most readily to mind.

Snipe inhabit a wide range of habitats that share only one common feature – water. With their extremely long bill they probe deep into mud for their food and are thus completely dependent on wetlands for their existence. Fortunately Canada abounds in such places and the Common Snipe is common indeed in many parts of the country. It breeds from British Columbia northwards well beyond the Arctic Circle to the Mackenzie Delta on the Beaufort Sea. Avoiding the more severe areas of tundra, it breeds right across the Northwest Territories to the southern shore of Hudson Bay and northwards across Quebec to Newfoundland and Nova Scotia. It extends southwards through the forested areas of Canada and right across the prairies to and beyond the International Border.

Throughout this huge range Snipe are summer visitors, the whole population moving southwards to winter throughout the United States, Mexico and Central America to South America where they mix freely with the birds that are resident almost throughout that continent. A few Snipe remain to winter with us in southern Ontario, in New Brunswick, Nova Scotia and Newfoundland and regularly along the coast and southern interior of British Columbia. The latter birds are dependent on open water created by hot springs.

Elsewhere in the world this same bird is found right across Europe and northern Asia as well as in southern and eastern Africa where, as in South America, it is resident. It winters in

the savannah lands south of the Sahara as well as throughout Asia. Though there are many distinct species of snipe in other parts of the world, this is the only one found in Canada.

Snipe are easy to identify though difficult to see. The long straight bill is about three times the length of the head and is used to probe deeply into soft mud in search of food. The upperparts are brown, heavily barred with black and streaked with cream to form a highly cryptic form of camouflage. This camouflage is aided by the bird's habit of standing stock still when alarmed. The head is dark brown, marked by a series of crown and facial stripes that effectively break up its outline. The underparts are white, variably barred with dark brown and with a wash of buff on the breast. Once picked out, the pattern of browns and creams and especially the long straight bill makes identification certain, but the birds are easily overlooked.

If approached too close they will leap into the air with a harsh *snark-snark* call and fly swiftly away with a typical zig-zag flight. In some parts of their range Snipe are a highly prized gamebird simply because of the skill required to shoot them, though they are also said to be very tasty and are regarded as a delicacy in France. Shooting is, however, confined to certain open seasons in winter when Snipe will gather into quite substantial flocks. In western Europe, where they winter as far north as Denmark and Scotland, heavy snow and freezing conditions trigger off hard weather movements that may bring many thousands together to milder areas of open water. There they probe virtually non-stop throughout the hours of daylight finding their prey by touch rather than sight and swallowing all except the largest food items without withdrawing their bill from the mud. They are also one of the most adaptable of birds and will quickly move to flooded areas in times of heavy rainfall. So when mild weather returns the flocks quickly disperse and move back to their original wintering areas.

Breeding Snipe stake out a territory that always includes its feeding grounds. The drumming flight of the male will, at first, encompass the whole of this area, but after pair formation drumming is centered on the female. Later, as the season progresses, it is concentrated on the male's favoured resting site. Males also display at other males on the ground making much of their boldly patterned tails which are spread vertically above their backs. Fights are frequent and males often come together breast to breast. They may also lie down, tail cocked, on the ground pointing their bills at rivals, and one even performed this threat display against a Red-winged Blackbird.

When a female has been attracted the male may dive at her from the air, on occasion turning completely upside down and even looping the loop. Though the sexes are similar and both equally well camouflaged, it is the female that performs the nesting duties. She constructs the nest on the ground using grasses to create a neat cup well hidden among damp tussocks. As with most other shorebirds, the usual clutch is four eggs, highly camouflaged in shades of olive or buff with spots and blotches of red-brown. Clutches of one to six are not unknown. Only a single brood is reared, though a new clutch will be laid to replace one that has been lost.

Common Snipe and chicks

Common Snipe
Gallinago gallinago

Pigeon Hawk
chasing Snipe

American
Woodcock

Eggs are laid at regular daily intervals and are incubated by the female for the eighteen to twenty days they take to hatch. She usually starts sitting when the clutch is complete, but sometimes with the second to last egg. As a result the chicks hatch at more or less the same time or separated by up to twenty-four hours. They leave the nest within a few hours of hatching and the male takes care of the older chicks leaving the female to continue with incubation and the care of the younger ones. At first they have comparatively short bills and are helped to feed by their parents, but they quickly grow and can fly after nineteen or twenty days. Though they can breed as one year olds, such birds often lay small clutches late in the season and some may not breed until their second year.

Though most Common Snipe migrate, several distinct subspecies have evolved over their huge range. Mostly they vary in size and coloration rather than pattern, so that separation in the field is virtually impossible. Some ornithologists even regard the birds that are resident in the southern hemisphere, in South America and Africa, as distinct species. The birds that breed throughout Canada belong to the subspecies *Gallinago gallinago delicata* which always has sixteen tail feathers. Many of our birds that breed in the east make a long migratory flight out over the Atlantic *en route* to South America. As a result some have been recovered in Bermuda and the Lesser Antilles and two have even been swept across the Atlantic to Britain in autumn.

Barn Swallow

The twittering of Swallows around our barns and homesteads in April is as welcome as the breath of spring itself. After their long, length of the continent journey, they are back and summer has arrived at last. They may gather on the wires and swoop low over the ponds in their search for insects, but within a few days they are busily exploring the barns and sheds where they nested the previous year. And yet it needs only a cold snap or a prolonged bout of wet weather for them to disappear and for us to think we are back in winter once more. In fact they probably have gone no further than the nearest marsh or lake where the insect food on which they depend may still be found. A couple of fine days and there they are again plastering mud to the beams or wall, building their first nest of the season.

Swallows are perfectly adapted to the life they lead. They are highly streamlined with a rounded head and thick body that tapers to a point. Their wings are long and sharply pointed making for fast and agile flight and their tails deeply forked to aid mobility. The bill is tiny, but it is backed by a huge gape that forms an effective funnel for scooping insects out of the air. The bird's upperparts are a dark blue-black, the underparts a buffy rufous, though the color of breast and belly vary enormously across its range. The forehead and neck are bright red, the latter bordered by a blue-black breast band. The tail is deeply forked and when spread shows a series of white spots. Male Swallows have longer tail streamers than females, while those of juveniles are shorter still. This enables a line of Swallows resting on a telegraph wire to be aged and sexed quite easily and, with a little practice, it is possible to tell whether it is a male or female that is coming and going with food for the young. Only the Cliff Swallow is at all similar, but that bird has a square tail as well as a pronounced rufous rump.

Barn Swallows breed right across Canada, though generally not far north of the tree line. They are thus absent from the northern Yukon, the Northwest Territories, northern Manitoba and the area of Hudson Bay and from much of

Barn Swallow
Hirundo rustica

Quebec and northern Newfoundland. Elsewhere they vary considerably in numbers being rare on the northern shores of the Gulf of St Lawrence and common in southern Ontario. They have, as their name implies, a close association with barns and other outbuildings and are thus far more abundant in areas of human settlement. As elsewhere in the world, the Barn Swallow must have benefitted considerably from man's inadvertent provision of nest sites, for before we constructed homes and houses across Canada the Swallow was dependent on caves.

Barn Swallows breed right across the United States southwards into Mexico and the whole of this population, as well as our Canadian birds, makes the long journey southwards each fall to spread throughout South America from Columbia to northern Argentina. The same species also breeds right across Europe and North Africa, through the Middle East and Siberia as far as Japan and China. The whole of this population moves southwards to winter in tropical and southern Africa and Asia as far south as New Guinea. European birds flying to winter quarters in Africa face one of the worst journeys in the world of birds. First they have to cross the Mediterranean, then, with little or no food from the narrow and parched coast of North Africa, set out across the Sahara

Desert. Many die on the way, but each year enough survive to bring a breath of spring to the farmers of Europe, from England to the Arctic coast of northern Norway.

Barn Swallows have one great advantage over many other small long-distance migrants – they feed in flight. They are therefore daytime migrants, feeding on the wing, then resting up for the night somewhere along the way. They are also highly gregarious and regularly spend the night at communal roosts in trees, bushes or for preference, reed beds. Huge flocks may sometimes gather at suitable roosts along the way as well as in their winter quarters. Yet though they move northwards together the flocks quickly break up once they have arrived and individuals become highly possessive about their nesting territory. Sometimes two or more pairs will share a farm between them, but the arrangement is never amicable and indicates no more than a shortage of nest sites.

The nest is constructed of pellets of mud, reinforced with grass and straw, built up over a period of several days. Each course of mud is allowed to dry before the next is added. Both members of the pair participate in the building, bringing mud from puddles or ponds nearby. Indeed, the availability of a suitable source of mud is an essential element in the Swallow's distribution. Eventually a shallow cup is created based on a

wide gape and
and broad bill base for
insect catching

beam or ledge inside a barn, garage, chicken shed or some such. The four to six eggs are round, white and speckled with reddish brown. They are incubated mainly, or perhaps entirely by the female for the fourteen to sixteen days they take to hatch. The young are born naked and helpless and are fed by both parents for about three weeks before fledging. At first their powers of flight are limited and they are fed by the adults for several more days before becoming independent. Soon, however, the adults are busily nest building again. Over most of their range Barn Swallows rear two broods, though in some places even a third may be raised. The youngsters band together and roam the neighbourhood before moving away.

Adult Swallows tend to return to the same site each year and will breed with their previous year's partner if available. This is by no means the rule, however, and divorces are far from uncommon. Young birds too return to the area where they were born, but are unlikely to use the same building. That Swallows occupy the same sites year after year does not indicate that the same birds are involved. It is more likely that a good site that has been used before will be used again.

Because they nest within the safety of buildings Barn Swallows have a high success rate and at the end of the breeding season their numbers are very high. Yet their hazardous migrations take an enormous toll with over eighty per cent of youngsters and sixty per cent of adults dying before the next spring. The chances of both members of a pair surviving are about one in five and of breeding together about one in ten. So the Swallows that return to the barn in spring are probably not those that occupied it last year, though it's nice to think that they might be and they are welcome nevertheless.

Barn Swallows feed mainly on insects that they find near the ground. They generally hunt at lower levels than other swallows and martins and considerably lower than swifts. In cold weather they often hawk for insects low over ponds and will even dip down to take an emerging insect from the surface film. They also drink on the wing, skimming across the water to scoop it up in their mouths with wings raised above their backs. Swallows also frequently feed around domestic animals, doubtless attracted by the hordes of flies that can be found in such circumstances.

The autumn gathering of Swallows on telegraph and power cables is a sign that winter is not so long away. At first such gatherings occur in the early evenings and are no more than a prelude to finding a satisfactory roost. Later they consist of birds ready for migration twittering to each other prior to setting out on their long journey south. They may rise, twittering madly, before returning, but eventually they will fly up and not return as they set out on a journey from which few will return.

Cliff Swallow

Tree Swallow

Black-billed Magpie

Though it is known simply as "The Magpie" throughout most of its range, this species is called the Black-billed Magpie in North America to distinguish it from the similar Yellow-billed Magpie. This latter bird is confined to the valleys and surrounding hills of California and is unknown in Canada. The Black-billed Magpie is widespread in the Old World, being found right across Europe and Asia from Britain to the Middle East, and Siberia to China and Kamchatka. It was doubtless from this latter area, just across the Bering Straits, that the species first arrived in the New World to settle in Alaska. A glance at its North American distribution clearly indicates a colonization from this direction, followed by a continued expansion of range southwards and eastwards. Just when this settlement of the west occurred it is impossible to say, but even today the Magpie is extending its range to both north and east.

At the present time Magpies breed from the southern Yukon through central British Columbia eastwards across most of Alberta and Saskatchewan to south and western Manitoba. Across the International Border they breed throughout the Rockies as far south as Nevada, though avoiding the milder climes of California. It thus seems unlikely that they will ever meet up with the Yellow-billed Magpie and compete with that strangely isolated species.

Though it appears a simple black and white bird at any distance, a close approach shows just what a colorful bird the Black-billed Magpie is. The darker feathers of wing and tail are, in fact, washed with an iridescent sheen of blue and green, while the tips of the tail feathers are burnished with gold and purple. The head, back and breast are black with a white belly and distinctive white patch on the wing. Though they appear black when folded, the primary flight feathers of the wing have white centres that flash as the bird flies. The most obvious feature is the rounded tail that is considerably longer than the body and is frequently cocked above the back.

Throughout its range the Magpie is a predator and scavenger. Not surprisingly this has brought it into sharp conflict with man in many areas and in Europe, in particular, it is ruthlessly persecuted by farmers and sportsmen alike. It will readily take the chicks and eggs of any bird it finds including gamebirds and feeds readily on the carcasses of young lambs, a habit which does little to endear it to sheep farmers. Yet, in the Far East, this same bird is held in high esteem and is often called "bird of joy."

Magpies feed mostly on the ground. They are practically omnivorous and will take insects and their larvae, small mammals, the eggs and young of birds, seeds, grain, fruit, berries and virtually anything edible discarded by man. They frequent rubbish tips, feed on road casualties – small mammals and other birds – and will fearlessly approach predators to help them finish off a carcass. Like the other crows, for the Magpie is related to the Crow, the Raven and our various jays, it hoards food by hiding it in the ground or in some crevice or hole. In this manner they have no doubt helped many a seed to germinate and tree to grow.

Though their distribution in Canada is essentially western, they occur in conifer forests and birch scrub as well as in the more open areas of the prairies. All that is really required is a sufficient growth of trees or bushes to provide them with a satisfactory nest site. If left in peace they will even move into farms virtually devoid of trees. The nest itself is usually situated in a tree or bush, seldom at any great height from the ground. In some places it is actually built on the ground itself and, outside Canada at least, even under the eaves of houses or atop a telegraph pole. It consists of a tightly knit ball of twigs

flight feather

Black-billed Magpie
Pica pica

with, wherever available, thorny spines as an added defence against predators. A side entrance hole leads to a mud-lined nesting chamber with a bed of roots or similar soft material including moss, leaves, hair and even rags to hold the eggs. In some areas the top canopy is not constructed and the nest left open to the elements. It is built by both members of the pair, often well before it is to be used.

The five or six, occasionally as many as ten, eggs are greenish blotched and spotted with shades of brown. The ground colour varies considerably and virtually unmarked blue eggs have been recorded. Incubation is by the female alone starting with the first egg. The male brings his mate food while she sits, as well as providing the bulk of food for the newly hatched chicks during the first few days of their lives. Some seventeen or eighteen days of sitting are required to hatch the eggs and a further twenty-two to twenty-seven days of feeding before the young fledge. Despite the attentions of the adults many nests are robbed, particularly by raccoons. Crows also attempt nest robbing, though they are generally only successful where the nest canopy has not been built.

Magpies are often gregarious forming loose flocks five to ten strong. These flocks are particularly noticeable in spring and may form an important prelude to breeding. Equally they may just be social. Certainly the birds form communal roosts in winter and often then gather in large numbers. It has been suggested that such regular meetings enable unpaired birds to meet up, though most other birds do not require such meetings to form pairs. Display is, however, a regular feature of these gatherings and both threatening and enticing displays make much use of the areas of white that are usually kept covered. Displaying birds also show off their magnificent tails to some effect, spreading them to flaunt the bright colors that glint in the light.

Young Magpies are frequently reared in captivity, perhaps because their ability to eat virtually anything makes them an easy prospect for the ordinary countryman. Such birds become accomplished mimics and will learn to produce actual words if taught to do so. In the wild they produce a rapid chattering as well as a variety of other calls.

Despite persecution the Black-billed Magpie is a very successful species. In Canada it continues to expand its range aided by a winter dispersal that regularly brings it into areas where it does not breed. In southern Europe it is abundant, while in Britain it is expanding rapidly into towns and even the centers of large cities. Just why the species should be enjoying such a boom remains unexplained, though man's activities within the countryside have undoubtedly increased the amount of suitable habitat as well as the quantity of food available. It seems only a matter of time before this beautiful bird, if somewhat unattractive in its habits, spreads right across Canada.

Grey Jay

Black-billed Magpie

Brown Creeper

The Brown Creeper breeds right across the southern half of Canada from Vancouver Island to southern Newfoundland. It is also found southwards through large areas of the United States, Mexico and even as far as Central America. In the Old World it extends from Britain across Europe, Russia and Siberia to Japan, with major outposts to the south in the Caucasus and Himalayas. Throughout this huge range it is confined to trees and is quite unknown in treeless tundra and open grasslands. Thus it is absent from the prairies of southern Alberta, Saskatchewan and south-western Manitoba as well as from the far north.

In the Old World the Brown Creeper is called the Treecreeper, but as there are several distinct species inhabiting that continent it is best known as the Common Treecreeper because of its huge range. There can be little doubt that our Canadian birds had their origin in Asia, but they crossed the Bering Straits a very long time ago, indeed when the two continents were joined by land.

At first glance the Brown Creeper is a rather dull-colored little bird that is easily overlooked among the trees. The upperparts, including the crown, are shades of buff and brown liberally streaked and spotted with cream. This creates a highly effective camouflage that enables the bird to merge perfectly with the bark of the large trees where it spends its life. The underparts are white with no more than a hint of cream or pale buff. There is a bold white eyebrow and a dark eyestripe. By far the most obvious feature is the bill that is long, thin and decurved and quite unlike that of other tree-climbing birds such as the woodpeckers, sapsuckers and nuthatches. Whereas these other arboreal birds find their food by hacking at the tree bark, Brown Creepers probe delicately into crevices to find the small creatures on which they depend.

They are well adapted to tree climbing, with strong legs and feet armed with sharp, long claws. Unlike the woodpeckers, they have the normal bird foot with three toes pointing

Brown Creeper
Certhia familiaris

The
Brown
Creeper

forwards and one backwards. The tail consists of strongly shafted feathers from which the barbs are worn away to give a pointed appearance to each feather and a rather ragged end to the tail. Like the woodpeckers, but unlike the nuthatches, the tail is used as a fulcrum to aid climbing.

The birds climb in a series of jerks that takes them upwards around the trunks of tall trees. Carefully and methodically they work their way over the bark searching every nook and cranny for food. At the first sign of danger they move round the tree out of sight and continue exploring on the other side. This is, no doubt, an effective way of hiding from predators, but it also hides them from binocular carrying birdwatchers and can be very frustrating. The most common indication of their presence is the high-pitched *tsit-tsit* call which, although similar to some of the chickadees and especially the kinglets, is quite distinct once learned. Indeed the ability to pick out the various calls of woodland birds can save many an hour of foot slogging and neck-ache.

Once discovered, the Brown Creeper may allow a close approach, but as it flies from the top of one trunk to the bottom of the next it effectively disappears. In flight it shows a bold buff bar across the wings. Such bars, in species such as the shorebirds for instance, are usually regarded as signals to other members of the flock, but in the Creeper it may serve to break up the bird's outline and confuse would-be predators in the dappled light.

Creepers feed mainly on insects and their larvae and take a wide variety of species including flies and moths in quantity. They also take various species of wasps, as well as spiders and their eggs and woodlice. Though weed seeds have been recorded, they form an insignificant part of the diet.

The birds nest beneath a piece of loose bark or among the debris of a broken off branch. The five or six white eggs are speckled with reddish-brown and laid in a neat cup lined with grass or roots. Incubation, which takes fourteen or fifteen days, is shared between the sexes and the young are cared for and fed by both members of the pair. Usually only a single brood is reared.

Winter Wren

"Winter Wren" is a particularly inept name for a bird that is present in Canada almost entirely in summer. Indeed, from a Canadian viewpoint "Summer Wren" would be a much better name. The name clearly has its origins south of the International Border for the birds that breed right across Canada flood southward in the fall and are widespread winter visitors to large areas of the eastern half of the United States. Elsewhere this Wren is found across the Bering Straits in Manchuria and northern Japan and in a broad band across Asia via the Himalayas to the Middle East and virtually the whole of Europe including Iceland. Over the whole of its Eurasian range it is the only species of wren, whereas in the Americas it is one of almost sixty species. Clearly then wrens had their origins in the New World and the Winter Wren has spread to the Old. Whether it was an eastward spread across the Atlantic via Iceland, or a westwards spread across the Bering Sea remains a subject of debate, though the latter seems much more likely when a land-bridge connected Asia and Alaska. What is clear is that its migratory habits and remarkable adaptability are responsible for making this one of the world's most successful small birds. Strange as it may seem the Wren is far more numerous in Europe than it is in its native Canada.

The Winter Wren is a tiny bird some $3\frac{3}{4}$ inches in length. It is a dark rust brown above, heavily barred with black, and buffy below barred, especially on the flanks, with brown. It has a pronounced white eyebrow, a longish decurved bill and a short tail that is invariably cocked vertically above its back. The legs and feet are strong and well developed. Its scientific name *Troglodytes troglodytes* reflects its skulking habits as well as

Winter Wren
Troglodytes troglodytes

House Wren

the fact that it breeds in holes often on the ground. A troglodyte is literally a cave-dweller. Though similar in appearance to the House Wren, it is smaller and has a much shorter tail than that bird. It also has a very distinctive song.

As with so many small, dull-colored and skulking birds, song is very important to the Winter Wren. It consists of varied phrases uttered at full volume that can be heard over half a mile away. Each version ends in a characteristic wheezing rattle. No matter where it lives the Wren belts out its song at full blast day after day. With such secretive habits volume is clearly necessary for individual birds to find each other. It also has a penetrating *tic-tic* that enables it to keep contact with others of its species at closer range.

Winter Wrens breed from southern Alaska through British Columbia, northern Alberta, central Saskatchewan and Manitoba. They extend eastwards through the southern half of Ontario and Quebec to New Brunswick and Nova Scotia to Newfoundland Island. They are absent from the prairies where the House Wren takes their place. Virtually all Winter Wrens leave Canada during the winter, though small numbers stay on in British Columbia and in the Great Lakes and St Lawrence region north to Nova Scotia. Western birds move southwards to California and mingle with resident Wrens, while eastern birds move south to the eastern and southern United States as far west as Texas.

In summer they are mostly birds of coniferous forests, though in their winter quarters they are also found in deciduous woodland. The basic requirement is a plentiful supply of undergrowth to cover their activities. No doubt this choice of habitat is partly a result of competition with other North American wrens, for in the Old World, where they are the only wren present, they occupy a wide range of different landscapes. There they are found in woods of both conifers and deciduous trees, but also in more open scrub country, along hedgerows, in suburban gardens and even city parks, on mountain sides up to 15,000 feet and on bare and isolated oceanic islands. Because of their ability to spread and colonize they have reached Iceland, the Faeroes, the Outer Hebrides including the remote rock of St Kilda, as well as the Shetland Isles. On each island group Wrens have become sufficiently isolated to form distinct subspecies, some of which are identifiable in the field.

130

Some of these island subspecies were in great demand for collections of both museums and individuals last century and suffered a serious decline as a result. When the famous ornithologist W. H. Hudson visited St Kilda in 1894 he was able to state that the endemic subspecies *Troglodytes troglodytes hirtensis* was now extinct. As a result a special amendment to the British Bird Protection Act of 1880 was passed, giving protection to this bird at a site where bird-killing had always been allowed because the small human population had always depended on "fowling" for food. Fortunately the St Kilda Wren was not extinct, but the amendment to the Act had the effect of creating a flourishing black market in the birds and their eggs, with prices reaching quite staggering figures. At the present time some 250 pairs of St Kilda Wrens now survive on these treeless islands.

Having staked out its territory by loud bouts of singing, and acquired a mate, the male Winter Wren constructs a series of nests in likely spots. These so-called "cock nests" are inspected by the female, that chooses one and adds her own lining. Such nests are usually placed in a hole among rocks, among the roots of a fallen tree, in an old broken stump, in a brush or wood pile, or even in a house or shed. It is a completely domed structure with a neat entrance hole at one side. The five or six white eggs are variably spotted with rusty-red, though both their number and coloration varies from place to place and from one subspecies to the next. The female performs fourteen or fifteen days of incubation unaided by her mate, though he joins her in feeding the chicks for the sixteen or seventeen days that they take to fledge. In many areas two broods are usually reared.

Wrens hunt for food on or near the ground and take large quantities of insects and their larvae. Indeed the chicks are fed almost entirely on a diet of moth caterpillars. They also take spiders as well as some seeds in winter. The hard season creates problems for all birds, but for those as small as the Winter Wren food is only one of many. Cold has a much greater effect on smaller birds than it does on larger ones and the Winter Wren has overcome the problem of heat loss by roosting communally. Several birds may regularly spend the night huddled together in a single safe hole and, in exceptional circumstances, no less than sixty-three Wrens have been counted entering a single chickadee nest box to roost.

132

Though it may suffer a severe decline in numbers in hard and prolonged winters, the Wren is quite capable of bouncing back very quickly. In Britain, where it is for the most part resident, numbers may be cut by half or more, yet within a couple of years they are back to normal. Indeed, the Winter Wren makes a more speedy recovery than virtually any other bird.

Though it is highly migratory in North America and suffers in hard weather everywhere, many populations of Winter Wrens in Europe are resident. In Britain there is only a small passage of birds from the extreme north, with most birds taking their chances with the winter. There are, however, some long distance recoveries of ringed birds up to 800 miles away, though this is nothing compared with the journeys of a thousand miles or more undertaken by many of our own birds.

Winter Wrens are nowhere very numerous in Canada, but their distinctive songs are a welcome sound of spring wherever they occur.

Common Starling

The Common Starling was first introduced to North America in 1890 when small numbers were released in New York City. There can be little doubt that this was one of the most foolish acts ever perpetuated in the history of our continent, and a prime example of what can happen when alien life forms are introduced to any new area. Within a century the Starling had spread throughout the United States, into northern Mexico and right across southern Canada. And it has not stopped yet. In other parts of the world it has been successfully introduced in Australia, New Zealand and South Africa, all areas where the colonizing English seemed to need reminders of home.

Starlings are natives of Europe and adjacent parts of Russia. They have spread southwards through the Middle East and eastwards to central Siberia. Their colonizations have been aided by being highly migratory and truly huge numbers leave the eastern and northern parts of their range to find milder climes in which to spend the winter. In many parts of Europe flock after flock can be watched flying westwards to the moist and mild west coast. Along the way they will gather in enormous roosts, some of which may be up to a million strong. Later in the winter, roosts are generally smaller, though the size is still dramatic.

In the late afternoon Starlings gather into large flocks that soon move off toward their roost in the safety of a reed bed or, more recently, in the warm center of a large city. Flocks arrive from all directions for distances up to twenty miles and form noisy swarms in trees adjacent to the roost site. They fly high into the air calling continuously, swooping and diving around the skies like a huge swarm of overlarge bees. If the swarm splits up birds left detached in the middle will fly to the nearest group while the "head" of the group turns to reconnect with those detached. Suddenly one part of the swarm will dive headlong toward the roost stretching the shape downwards until a break occurs and the swarm turn upwards again. The process is then repeated again and again until, with a final surge, all the remaining birds dive down together to the safety of the roost.

By any standards this is a spectacular performance and probably the most dramatic that most of us will ever see from wild birds. The noise attracts predators and the regularity with which Starlings use the same site makes them easy prey. Peregrines and Pigeon Hawks, in particular, regularly lie in ambush at Starling roosts and are seldom disappointed. Their impact, however, is negligible.

During the Second World War pioneer radar watchers were bedevilled by 'angels' that kept appearing on their screens but seemingly did not exist. In particular they kept finding rings appearing in the early mornings, rings that spread outwards from a single point like the rings of water created by dropping a stone into a pond. Investigation showed that the rings were successive waves of Starlings leaving their roost in the early mornings when birds fanned out over the surrounding countryside. Modern radar, it is reassuring to know, is "angel-free."

Some of the most famous roosts are those in the centers of large cities, though these are generally not as large as country roosts. City centers are several degrees warmer than the surrounding countryside and Starlings will flock into parks and squares with considerable risk to those below. Their droppings coat the buildings on which they spend the night and they may form a potential health hazard. Where public authorities have made efforts to deter the birds from the habit, the swarms have usually moved a few hundred yards and created the same problem elsewhere. There is, it seems, little that can be done about the Starling problem.

The success of the Starling is, in no small measure, due to its ability to live alongside man. Indeed, there is hardly a single human activity that does not in some way seem to benefit these highly adaptable birds. Wherever man has changed the countryside there will be a healthy population of Starlings. As we have seen warm city centers attract them to roost and our rubbish tips offer a plentiful supply of scraps as food. They come to bird feeding stations, often driving away the species for which the food was actually intended. They gather at sewage works and are one of the few species that have learned to feed on modern sprinkler systems, hopping over or perching on the rotating arms. They frequently nest in holes in buildings and will quickly fill a disused chimney with sticks to form a basis for their nests. Many a weekender has found it

Common Starling
Sturnus vulgaris

impossible to light a fire at his country retreat because Starlings have blocked the chimney during his absence. They will take over the nest holes of other species and in this way have been largely responsible for the decline of our Red-headed Woodpecker and probably also of the Bluebird. They will also take over nest boxes intended for other species. All in all they are a menace that causes considerable damage wherever they are found.

Despite this Starlings are attractive and interesting birds. In summer they are a fine iridescent blue-black on head and underparts with the black feathers of back and wing broadly edged with buff-brown. The legs are pinkish-red and the bill a bright yellow. In winter the whole body is heavily spotted with buff and the bill becomes slate-gray. Juveniles are a dirty buffy-gray marked by a white chin, but this plumage is gradually replaced by the spotted winter plumage during the late summer. On the ground Starlings walk with a distinctive waddling action. In the air they fly fast and direct, their short tails giving them a quite different flight shape to the thrushes, similar only to the waxwings among our native birds.

Starlings are hole nesters and doubtless were at one time most common in woodland where they utilized natural holes as well as the disused holes of woodpeckers. Even today large numbers of birds still breed in woods, though because of their aggressiveness and increased population they now usurp woodpeckers from holes they have barely finished excavating. Both members of the pair bring the nest material which consists of twigs, grasses, straw, feathers and any other rubbish they can find such as polythene and paper. The nest is an untidy structure and debris is often left trailing from the hole. The five or six eggs, sometimes up to nine, are pale blue, occasionally almost white, and are incubated for eleven to fourteen days, mainly, though not exclusively, by the female. Both sexes bring food to the young, though the female brings the larger share, for the twenty to twenty-two days that they take to fledge. Though most Starlings are single-brooded, second broods are not at all unusual and may be the rule in some areas.

During the summer Starlings take mostly animate food, including large quantities of insect pests and their larvae from agricultural ground. This is almost their only saving grace. Beetles, weevils, slugs, snails, centipedes, woodlice as well as spiders and earthworms have all been recorded. At other seasons vegetable matter is more important and this includes cereals, fruit and fruit buds, potatoes, seeds and berries. Overall their diet is more or less equally divided between vegetable and animal matter.

Starlings first colonized Canada when birds arrived at Niagara Falls in the fall of 1914. By December of the following year they were at Halifax, Nova Scotia and within eighteen months were at Betchouane, Quebec. They spread through the east reaching New Brunswick in 1924 and Prince Edward Island in 1930 and were as far west as Manitoba by 1931. The first record for Alberta followed in 1934 with Saskatchewan in 1937. Newfoundland was reached in 1943 and British Columbia in 1945. They now breed right across Canada from southern Vancouver Island to Newfoundland and as far north as northern Alberta and James Bay. In the United States they have covered the entire country. Though Starlings winter throughout their Canadian breeding range, many move southwards at this time of the year.

House Sparrow

The House Sparrow is a native of Europe and Asia that has been introduced to many parts of the world and has flourished. It is now familiar in every large landmass and continues to expand its range. Though called a "sparrow" it is not closely related to our native sparrows, being, in fact, a weaverbird with many relatives in Africa and Asia. It was first introduced to North America in Brooklyn, New York in 1850 and later to Halifax and Quebec. From these humble beginnings it has spread right across the settled areas of Canada from Vancouver Island to Nova Scotia, and is now a common bird of both town and country.

In the United States it spread westwards with amazing rapidity reaching California within forty years of the first few being released in New York. This was not the result of a migration, for House Sparrows are generally resident. The birds simply bred, prospered and spread outwards. Partly this is the result of their remarkable capacity to breed virtually throughout the year and certainly of their ability to rear several broods each summer. More important is their relationship with man for, though they once must have existed without our aid, they are now almost totally dependent on us for their livelihood.

Like that other successful colonist the Starling, House Sparrows are hole nesters and will readily take to nest sites created by or for other species. Mostly they nest in holes in buildings, but they will readily take to nest boxes and frequently usurp the nests of swallows and martins. They often take over the nests of Tree Swallows and are a major threat to the Cliff Swallow that is suffering a serious decline, almost certainly due to competition with the aggressive and pugnacious House Sparrow.

These birds are often semi-colonial, requiring only a nest site and an adjacent perch as a territory. They are particularly fond of holes under the eaves of buildings, but will also construct an untidy ball of grass and straw in a bush if holes are short, but food is plentiful. Food is, in fact, the determining

House Sparrow
Passer domesticus

factor in the spread and range of the Sparrow for it is seldom found far from human habitation. In Europe, where House Sparrows range as far north as the North Cape of Norway, they are absent from areas where human occupation is only seasonal. In these situations their place is taken by the White Wagtail. Also in Europe they suffered one of their greatest setbacks when horse-drawn transport, with its inevitable grain spillage, was replaced by the automobile. In London numbers actually declined, though to visit that city today one would hardly imagine so.

Elsewhere in the world House Sparrows have been introduced in South America and have spread from Tierra del Fuego to Peru and southern Brazil. They are widespread in South Africa as well as in Australia and New Zealand, and it seems quite likely that they will eventually occupy every city and town in the world. All this within a hundred and fifty years of the first introductions shows the incredible adaptability of this little bird.

House Sparrows are really quite attractive. The male is a bright chestnut on the back marked by black streaking and a bold white wing bar. The crown is gray, the ear coverts white, and a black bib extends from the chin to the upper breast. The underparts are a buffy-gray. The female is rather duller in buffs and browns, but with a marked buffy eyebrow. Colors vary enormously across their range, and even in North America paler or darker birds tend to predominate in certain areas. Some of these are so marked that ornithologists have even been tempted to regard them as separate subspecies in areas where they have been established for less than 150 years.

In spring Sparrows perform a communal display with a group of loudly chirruping males displaying to a single female. Wings drooped and tails raised, they scuffle around the female. When she flies away all will follow. The male builds his nest and then chirrups away nearby to attract a mate and proclaim his ownership. Once a pair is established both birds will join in the work of finishing the nest. The two to seven gray eggs are spotted and blotched with black. Birds in New Zealand usually lay four eggs, while those in North America lay five. Older birds usually lay more eggs than young ones, and it may be that larger clutches than normal in North America indicate a greater preponderance of older birds and a higher level of survival.

The twelve to fourteen days of incubation are mainly performed by the female, though the male takes a share when the eggs are close to hatching and may perform up to half during the last day or two. Both parents feed the chicks and, though containing a larger proportion of insects, the food is more or less the same as that eaten by the adults themselves. In cities broods may be reared on a diet consisting almost entirely of bread. In larger clutches hatching may be spread over two days, leaving one or more of the chicks much smaller than the others. Such runts invariably obtain less than their fair share of food and usually die. The chicks fly after eleven to eighteen days depending on the quality and availability of food. A second clutch is laid about ten days after the young of the previous brood have flown. Three or four broods are reared in temperate regions, though only one or two in the arctic parts of their range.

At the end of the breeding season House Sparrows often become quite scarce around their nesting sites. Large flocks gather in more open countryside, quite independent of buildings, to raid the hedgerows and particularly fields of cereals. Large quantities of grain are taken both before and after harvest much to the annoyance and financial loss of farmers. Later, when the bonanza is over, Sparrows return to their scavenging tactics around our houses and farms for the winter. Though large numbers die every year this is merely the surplus population produced by a high reproductive rate and an autumn food glut.

In the depths of winter we keep the population going by regularly feeding the birds. We may not intend to feed the Sparrows, but it is difficult to devise a Sparrow-proof feeder and, in any case many people quite like Sparrows. In the later winter and spring the birds turn their attention to our gardens and regularly nip off the buds of shrubs and fruit trees. It is this remarkable adaptability, the ability to exploit a range of different foods and feeding styles, that is responsible for the continued success of the House Sparrow. There seems little that we can do that will limit their increase and spread.

Over most of its range the House Sparrow is resident, though young birds may move a hundred miles or so. In Asia, where there is no tradition of bird feeding and the winters are as harsh as our own, the birds actually migrate out of northern Iran and Afghanistan to winter on the plains of India and Pakistan. These movements bring them into contact with local flocks and together they roam the fertile plains in search of food.

Sharp-shinned hawk
attacking House Sparrow

Golden-crowned Kinglet

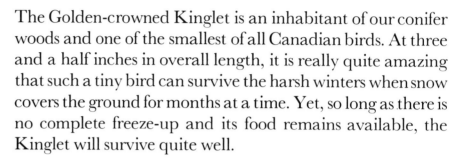

The Golden-crowned Kinglet is an inhabitant of our conifer woods and one of the smallest of all Canadian birds. At three and a half inches in overall length, it is really quite amazing that such a tiny bird can survive the harsh winters when snow covers the ground for months at a time. Yet, so long as there is no complete freeze-up and its food remains available, the Kinglet will survive quite well.

Among North American birds its closest relative is the Ruby-crowned Kinglet, though it is easily distinguished from that species. The Ruby-crowned breeds even further north than the Golden-crowned, its northern limit coinciding with the tree line. It does, however, migrate long distances southwards leaving Canada completely in winter. The Golden-crowned too is a migrant, but large numbers winter right across the southern parts of the country.

There are, in fact, only four species of kinglet in the world – two in North America and two in Eurasia. These latter are the Goldcrest and Firecrest, both of which closely resemble the Golden-crowned Kinglet. Indeed, the similarity between Firecrest and Golden-crowned Kinglet led to them being regarded as a single species at one time. Certainly these two birds are closely related, but their ranges are difficult to explain. If the distribution of Firecrest and Golden-crowned Kinglet are plotted on a world map it will be seen that there is a group in North America, another in Europe with isolated populations in Mexico and the Chinese island of Formosa. Such isolation would seem almost impossible and the present view that there are two, perhaps three distinct species seems much more feasible. In the unlikely event of a Firecrest flying the Atlantic, birdwatchers along our east coast watchpoints would be hard put to tell the difference.

The Golden-crowned Kinglet breeds from the southern coasts of Alaska, through southern Yukon to British Columbia and northern and western Alberta. It is absent

from the prairies, but extends eastwards from central Manitoba across Ontario and southern Quebec to New Brunswick, Nova Scotia and Newfoundland Island. In the United States it can be found through the mountains of the west coast as well as in the eastern Rockies almost to the Mexican border, though in these areas it is very much a high altitude bird. It is absent from the center of the States, but is also found in the northeast extending southwards through the Appalachians. In winter it moves southwards, though it remains to winter in British Columbia, southern Alberta, Saskatchewan, Manitoba, Ontario and Quebec as well as along the east coast north to Newfoundland.

The Golden-crowned Kinglet is dark olive-green above with a darker tail and black wings liberally edged with white. It has a bold double white wingbar, but this feature is shared with all three other kinglets. The underparts are pale, almost white with a flush of green along the flanks. The head pattern is both obvious and distinctive, consisting of a bright red coronal stripe bordered by bright yellow and black. There is a prominent white eyebrow and a black eyestripe and moustachial streak. The female differs only in lacking the red central crown stripe, her crown being marked only with yellow and black. Juveniles lack the crown stripe altogether.

Ruby-crowned Kinglet

Red-breasted Nuthatch

Kinglets spend much of their time high up among the branches of conifers and are easily overlooked. Though they fly from tree to tree and branch to branch and are hyperactive in their search for food, they are so small that it needs a sharp eye to pick them out. They are most often found by their high-pitched *zee-zee-zeet* calls that are similar in pitch and quality to those of chickadees and particularly to the Brown Creeper. The sound is, however, much thinner and once learned are quite distinct. Once a calling party has been located it is simply a matter of patience and searching to find the birds.

The birds are gregarious throughout the year, often associating with roving parties of small birds dominated by chickadees. They feed by searching out insects and their eggs and larvae among the pine needles and from bark crevices. The wings are flicked almost continually as they flit from twig to twig ever active in their search for food. Because they weigh only a sixth of an ounce, their high metabolic rate means that they have to feed all day long to survive.

In spring the male sings a song that consists of the first part of the call note followed by a twittering of descending notes similar to that of a chickadee. He also displays to his mate by fluffing out his body and making much of his colorful crest. The nest is a domed structure beautifully woven from moss, lichen and roots lined with feathers. It is usually situated high in a conifer, but may be at no great distance from the ground and is often suspended beneath one of the outermost twigs. It is constructed by both members of the pair. The five to ten eggs, more usually eight or nine, are white, spotted with buffy-brown. Incubation is by the female alone and lasts for fourteen to seventeen days, a surprisingly long period for so small a bird. The chicks are fed by both parents for 16 to 21 days. The Golden-crowned Kinglet is probably double-brooded.

As fall sets in many of our birds migrate southwards to seek milder climes. At this time they may be found in areas devoid of conifers and then feed among deciduous trees and bushes sometimes in association with warblers and Ruby-crowned Kinglets. In Eurasia Firecrests and Goldcrests are also partial migrants that frequently occur together during passage periods. In winter quarters the Golden-crowned is once more usually found in conifers, while the Ruby-crowned is much more frequent in deciduous woodland.

Golden-crowned Kinglet
Regulus satrapa

Bird Anatomy
Skeleton

Most aspects of the anatomy of birds are governed by their ability to fly. A strong but lightweight skeleton, powerful flight muscles and the outer distinctive covering of feathers.

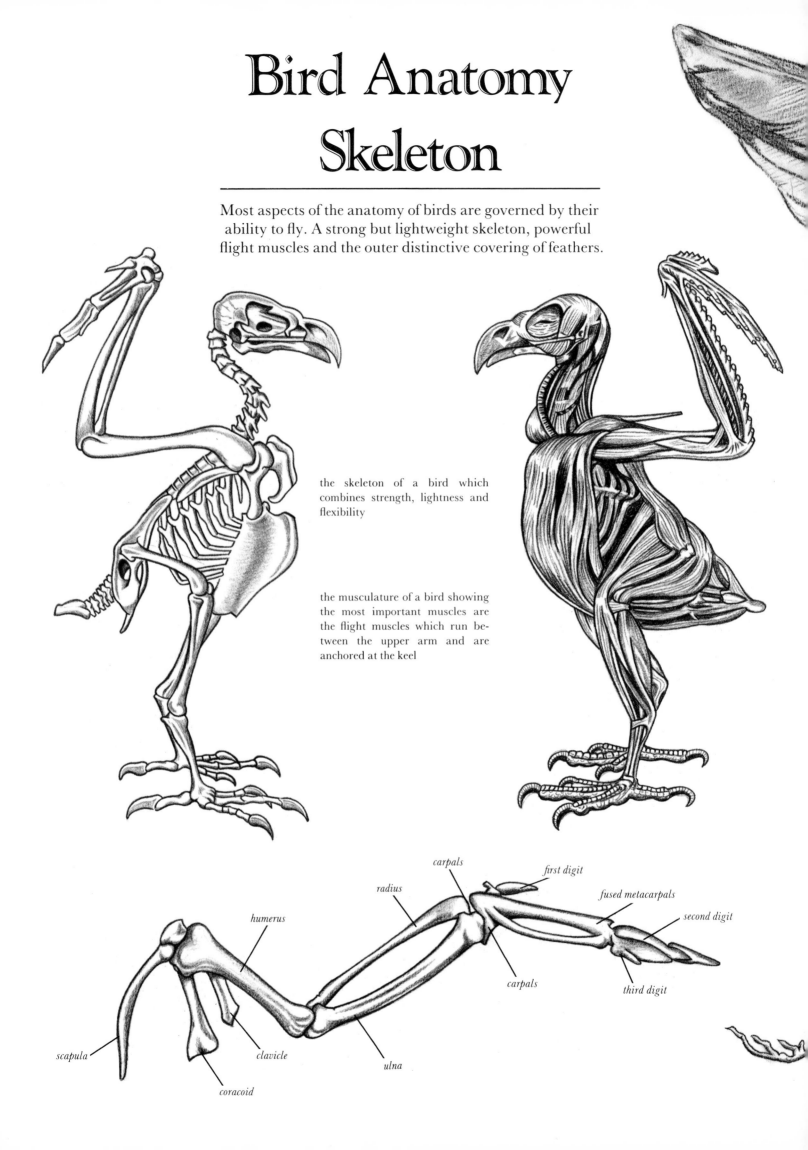

the skeleton of a bird which combines strength, lightness and flexibility

the musculature of a bird showing the most important muscles are the flight muscles which run between the upper arm and are anchored at the keel

carpals

radius

first digit

humerus

fused metacarpals

second digit

carpals

third digit

scapula

ulna

clavicle

coracoid

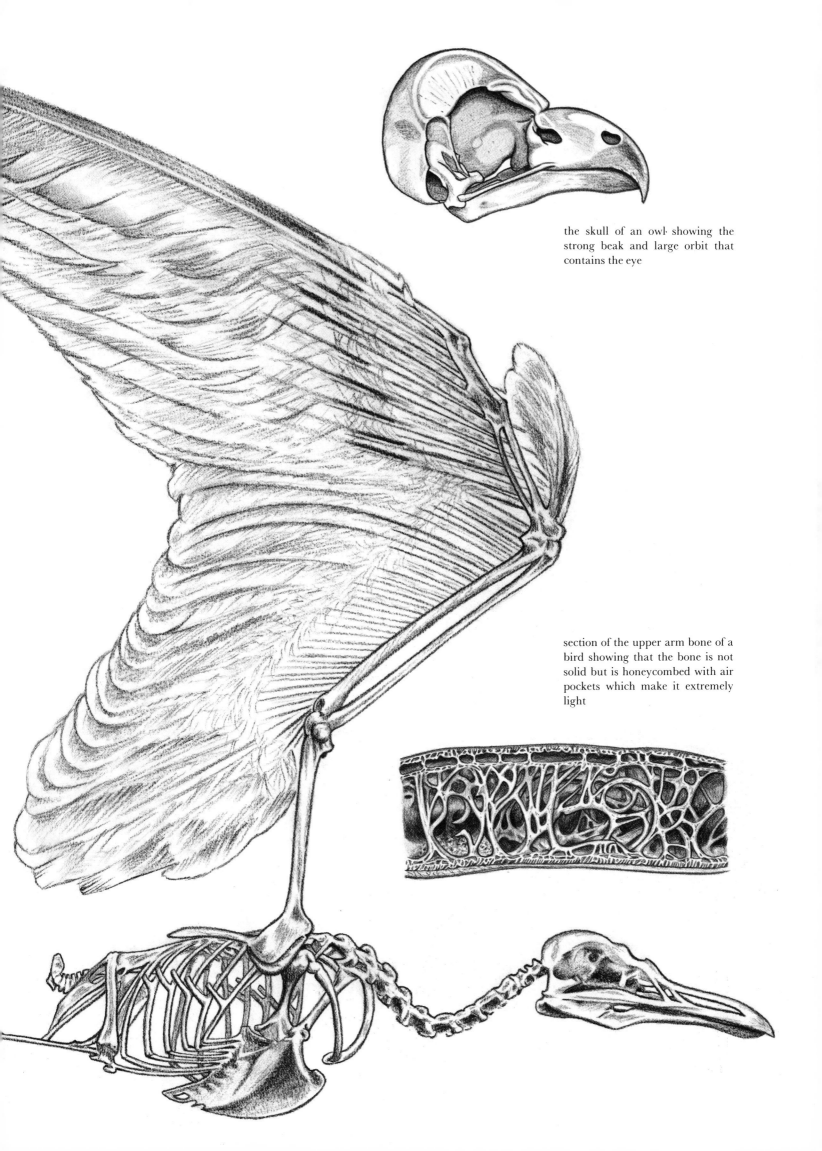

the skull of an owl showing the strong beak and large orbit that contains the eye

section of the upper arm bone of a bird showing that the bone is not solid but is honeycombed with air pockets which make it extremely light

Feathers

The most important single factor in
the bird's design for flight is the
feather, it is a marvel of natural
engineering extremely light
and structurally strong
it is easily replaced
when damaged
or broken

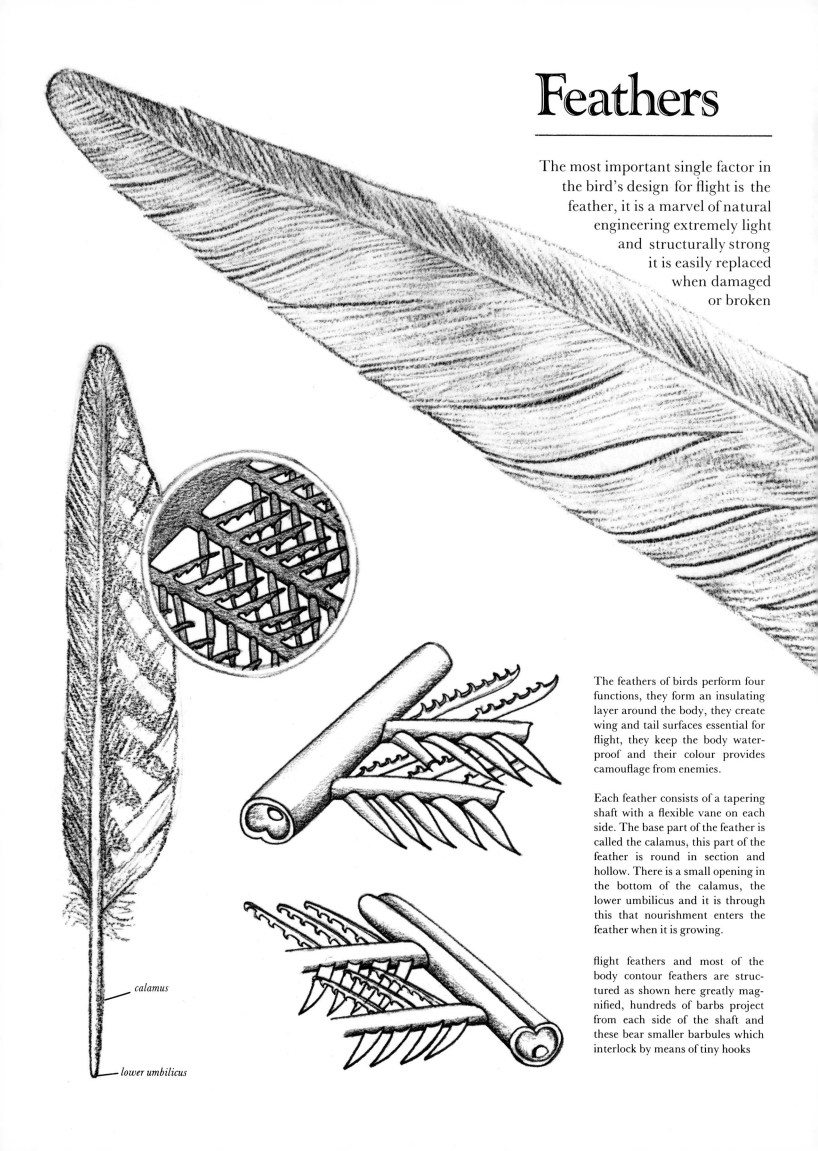

calamus

lower umbilicus

The feathers of birds perform four
functions, they form an insulating
layer around the body, they create
wing and tail surfaces essential for
flight, they keep the body water-
proof and their colour provides
camouflage from enemies.

Each feather consists of a tapering
shaft with a flexible vane on each
side. The base part of the feather is
called the calamus, this part of the
feather is round in section and
hollow. There is a small opening in
the bottom of the calamus, the
lower umbilicus and it is through
this that nourishment enters the
feather when it is growing.

flight feathers and most of the
body contour feathers are struc-
tured as shown here greatly mag-
nified, hundreds of barbs project
from each side of the shaft and
these bear smaller barbules which
interlock by means of tiny hooks

secondary coverts

smaller contour feathers

greater coverts

the powerful wing of a buzzard

primary feathers

secondary feathers

Bobwhite flank feather

Willow Grouse

Prairie Chicken scapular

Gray Partridge scapular

a variety of feather types

the long quill is a flight feather

the semi-plume is part vaned and part downy feather

the filoplume is a hair-like feather with a vestige of barbs

the down feather has a minute central shaft and fluffy barbs

Flight

The ability to fly is the most important asset a bird owns. It enables it to search or hunt for food, to escape from its enemies and to migrate to a climate and habitat that suits its particular needs

diagram to show the perfect balance of golden eagle standing and in flight

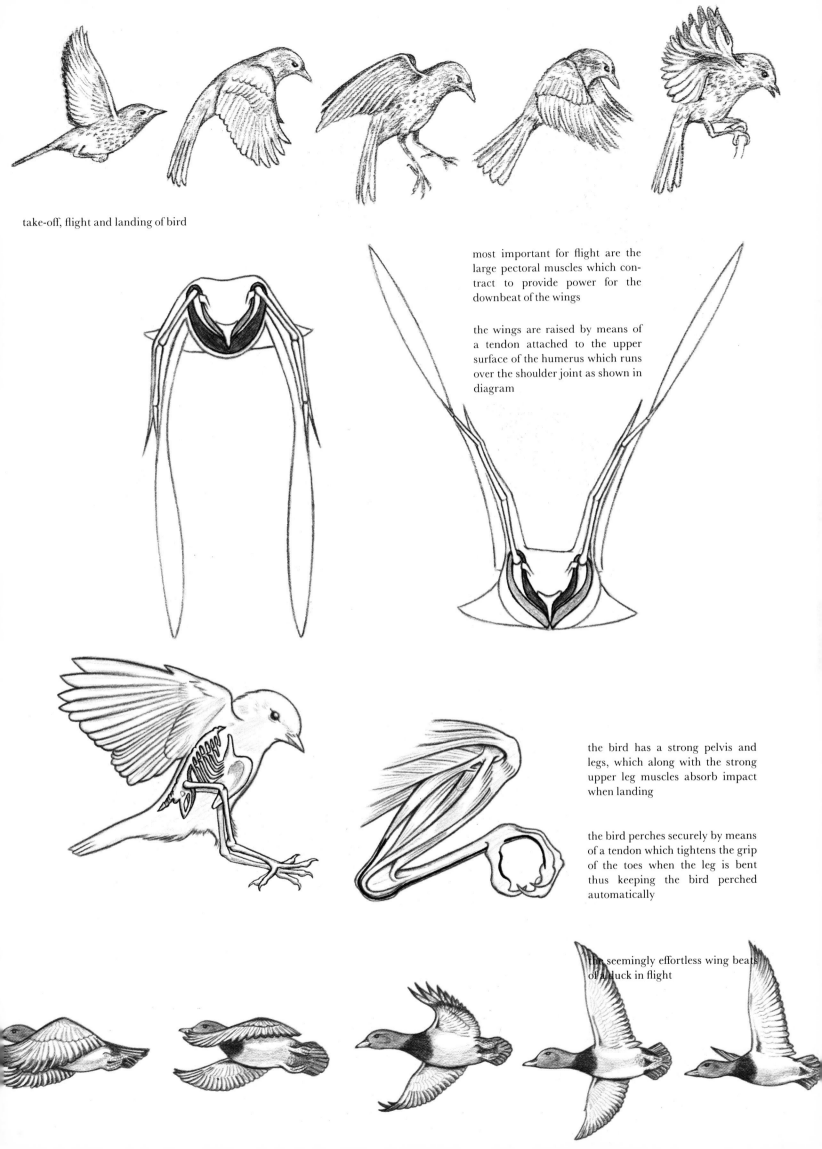

take-off, flight and landing of bird

most important for flight are the large pectoral muscles which contract to provide power for the downbeat of the wings

the wings are raised by means of a tendon attached to the upper surface of the humerus which runs over the shoulder joint as shown in diagram

the bird has a strong pelvis and legs, which along with the strong upper leg muscles absorb impact when landing

the bird perches securely by means of a tendon which tightens the grip of the toes when the leg is bent thus keeping the bird perched automatically

the seemingly effortless wing beats of a duck in flight

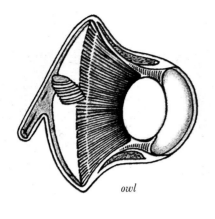

owl

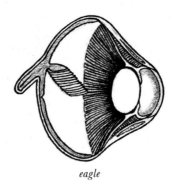

eagle

goose

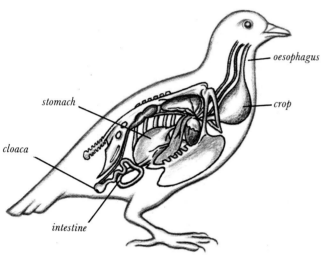

oesophagus

crop

stomach

cloaca

intestine

Bird's eyes in section showing different shapes, many birds have more acute eyesight than any other animal including man

the bird's internal organs viewed from the side. The digestive system is composed of an oesophagus which leads to the crop and a stomach which is divided into two chambers, the proventriculus and gizzard, the intestine runs to the cloaca which is an exit for the waste products, the cloaca also extracts water from the waste products

newly hatched chick

Common Snipe and chicks

Breeding

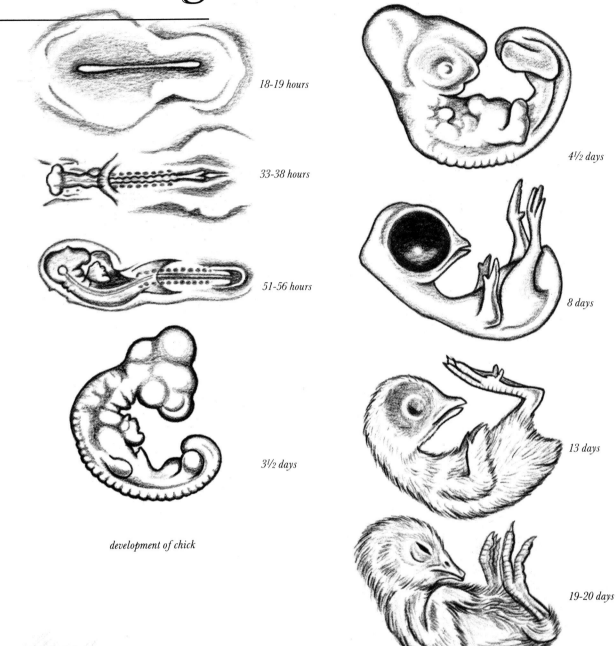

18-19 hours

33-38 hours

51-56 hours

3½ days

development of chick

4½ days

8 days

13 days

19-20 days

Hatching

the hard shelled eggs of birds are well known, they consist of three main parts, yolk, albumen and shell

the yolk is rich in fats and proteins on which the developing embryo feeds, the embryo floats on the yolk surrounded by the egg white or albumen which consists mainly of water. As shown the young chick develops very quickly and hatch at between 11 days in small birds and up to 12 weeks in very large birds

Select Bibliography

Ruffed
Grouse
tail feather

Gray
Partridge
scapular

Brown, Leslie and Amadon, Dean: *Eagles, Hawks and Falcons of the World*: London, 1968

Burton, Philip and Boyer, Trevor: *Vanishing Eagles*: London 1983

Coles, Charles and Pledger, Maurice: *Game Birds*: London 1983

Cramp, S. and Simmons, K. E. L.: *Birds of the Western Palearctic*: Oxford 1977, 1982

Gabrielson, Ira N. and Lincoln, Frederick C.: *Birds of Alaska*: Washington 1959

Godfrey, W. Earl: *The Birds of Canada*: Ottawa 1966

Gooders, John: *Birds of the World*: London 1969, 1971

Gooders, John: *Birds That Came Back*: London 1983

Keith, Stuart and Gooders, John: *Collins Bird Guide*: London 1980

Palmer, Ralph S.: *Handbook of North American Birds*: New Haven 1962, 1976

Peterson, Roger Tory: *A Field Guide to the Birds*: Boston 1934

Peterson, Roger Tory: *A Field Guide to Western Birds*: Boston 1941

Peterson, Roger Tory and others: *A Field Guide to the Birds of Britain and Europe*: London 1954

Robbins, Chandler S. and others: *Birds of North America*: New York 1966

Snyder, L. L.: *Arctic Birds of Canada*: Toronto 1957

Sprunt, Alexander Jnr: *North American Brids of Prey*: New York 1955

Thomsom, A. Landsborough: *A New Dictionary of Birds*: London 1964

Voous, K. H.: *Lists of Recent Holarctic Bird Species*: London 1977

Welty, Carle: *The Life of Birds*: Philadelphia 1962

Witherby, H. F. and others: *The Handbook of British Birds*: London 1938, 1942

Acknowledgements

Bobwhite
flank feather

Willow
Grouse

Californian
Quail
flank feather

This book is truly a co-operative effort in every sense of the word. It could not have been produced without the aid of two of the finest bird artists painting today. In Maurice Pledger's work we can see a finesse that evokes the wild places. His paintings evoke the very spirit of the bird. Trevor Boyer is equally outstanding, though in a different way. Just as eagles and birds of prey are different from game and garden birds, so is Trevor's art different from Maurice's. Here we have an artist whose attention to detail is second only to his knowledge of birds, especially of birds of prey, His portraits of these majestic birds are quite outstanding and are among the very best we have ever seen. Few authors are fortunate enough to work with one great bird artist; in this book I have been blessed with two. Alongside their work, my words are no more than an accompaniment.

My thanks are also due to Hubert Schaafsma whose idea this book was, and I have more than a passing suspicion that Bernard Thornton was not a million miles away at the time. Sophie Hale, of Dragon's World, is totally responsible for ensuring that my part in it was delivered on time, while Robert Morton drew the additional illustrations, to complement Trevor and Maurice's fine plates. Grant Bradford did the tricky task of the anatomical illustrations, as well as turning text and illustrations into the beautifully designed book that eventually materialized.

Finally, I must thank Robbie Chapman for producing a typescript from my often illegible manuscript, mostly before the ink was dry. She shared with me the birth pangs of *Birds of Canada*.